The Politics of English in Puerto Rico's Public Schools

THE POLITICS OF ENGLISH IN PUERTO RICO'S PUBLIC SCHOOLS

Jorge R. Schmidt

FIRST**FORUM**PRESS

A DIVISION OF LYNNE RIENNER PUBLISHERS, INC. • BOULDER & LONDON

Published in the United States of America in 2014 by
FirstForumPress
A division of Lynne Rienner Publishers, Inc.
1800 30th Street, Boulder, Colorado 80301
www.firstforumpress.com

and in the United Kingdom by
FirstForumPress
A division of Lynne Rienner Publishers, Inc.
3 Henrietta Street, Covent Garden, London WC2E 8LU

© 2014 by Lynne Rienner Publishers, Inc. All rights reserved

Library of Congress Cataloging-in-Publication Data
A Cataloging-in-Publication record for this book
is available from the Library of Congress.
ISBN: 978-1-935049-94-4

British Cataloguing in Publication Data
A Cataloguing in Publication record for this book
is available from the British Library.

This book was produced from digital files prepared by the author
using the FirstForumComposer.

Printed and bound in the United States of America

 The paper used in this publication meets the requirements
of the American National Standard for Permanence of
Paper for Printed Library Materials Z39.48-1992.

5 4 3 2 1

*To Ana María, my muse, friend, and beloved wife.
To Sofía and Alejandro, my dream children come true.
To Lolita, my mother, a real superhero.*

Contents

List of Tables and Figures ix

1 The Politics of Education and Language 1
2 The Educational Language Gap 21
3 Who's in Charge? 31
4 The English Question 47
5 Uses of English in Puerto Rico 69
6 Language Stakeholders 97
7 The Implications of Language Diversity 149

Bibliography *159*
Index *171*

Tables and Figures

Tables

2.1	Language Social Use	25
2.2	Categories of Language Social Use	26
2.3	Educational Language Use	27
2.4	Categories of Educational Language Use	28
5.1	English Educational Policies in Puerto Rico	94
6.1	Pivotal Circular Letters	100
6.2	Constitutional Duties of Education Commissioners	105
6.3	P.R. Education Budget, 1900–1923	113
6.4	P.R. Teachers' Monthly Salaries	118

Figures

1.1	Types of Decisionmaking in Educational Systems	15
5.1	English Social Use in Puerto Rico	70
5.2	English Educational Use in Puerto Rico	78
5.3	English ELAG in Puerto Rico	91
5.4	Uses of English in Puerto Rico	92

1
The Politics of Education and Language

This book is about the politics of language in education. It concerns the people who try to influence educational language policies and the institutions where those policies are determined. Now, most people would claim that politics are bad for education. Politics, they could add, contaminate the educational process and impose policy decisions that have little to do with pedagogic philosophy and much to do with power relations. Thus, many propose that politics should be removed altogether from educational policies, especially those relating to the language of instruction. Many have tried; none have succeeded. That is because, contrary to popular belief, politics is an indispensable component of public education.

Public education is political for two reasons. First, it is a powerful tool of socialization only surpassed by the family. Second, it involves several societal sectors with diverse and sometimes conflicting interests. The attempts to purge politics from education have failed in the past and will fail in the future. The goal should be the understanding, rather than the removal, of politics in educational policies, which are complex and multidimensional. This book concentrates on educational language policy, a crucial component of any public education system.

Politics is also a fundamental aspect of language. Language, as a social instrument of communication, control, and subversion, is essentially political because of its diversity. All countries face some level of language diversity, which presents policymakers with the dilemma of having to choose between uniformity and variety. The complexity of government operations provides incentives for state officials to simplify and pursue the establishment of a single language, a process known as language rationalization (Laponce, 1987). However, ethnolinguistic groups often demand policies that promote the use of several languages in their societies. Consequently, there exists a tension between the centralizing tendency of government bureaucracies and the centrifugal force of language diversity.

Given that public education and language contact contain by definition political dynamics, the formulation of educational language policies is, by consequence, a highly politicized process. For instance, most colonial governments imposed the center's language in official affairs and public education. They did so as part of a political project. Such was the case of Spanish and French colonial policies in the New World and Africa. Education and language also have been major issues in sovereign multilingual states, where language policies frequently have favored the groups with closer ties to the state and greater capacity to influence government decisions. Where those with the strongest influence over language policies constitute numerical minorities, the resulting educational language policies emphasize their languages at the expense of other languages. English in the Philippines, Swahili in Tanzania, English in Puerto Rico, Urdu in Pakistan, and Afrikaans in South Africa illustrate the point. In such cases, a gap may develop between the educational and the social uses of languages, which may in turn reinforce existing socioeconomic and political differences among language groups. Thus, educational language policies constitute important political and economic tools, and the power relations that create them must be examined.

Educational language policies result from the refraction of individuals' and groups' interests through the institutions of the educational system. Those individuals and groups act as language stakeholders, people who invest time and resources, expecting to increase their influence over educational language policies. The term is an adaptation of Samuel Popkin's "political entrepreneur," who is "someone willing to invest his own time to coordinate the inputs of others in order to produce collective action or collective goods" (1979:259). This book analyzes the policy preferences of those language stakeholders regarding the medium of instruction in public schools. McGroarty (2002:33) argued that language policies were undertheorized and that "practical decisions regarding language are made by the various groups wielding power within educational governance structures...." This work provides a theoretical, empirical and historical contribution on how those decisions come to be.

The language stakeholders' efforts to influence educational policy are channeled through the educational governance structures. Educational institutions affect the outcomes. They do so according to two fundamental attributes of those structures: centralization and participation. Centralization refers to the level at which policies are determined, from central educational ministries to local school boards and individual schools. Participation refers to the degree of involvement of teachers, parents, students, and the community in educational policies.

Education and Politics

The political nature of public education can be illustrated at least in four areas: (1) state formation, (2) political socialization, (3) class cleavages and (4) class formation.

The formation of modern states during the industrial revolution rested partly on the creation of mass educational systems. Anderson (1991) ascribed the development of nation-states in Europe to the emergence of "print-capitalism," which was the combination of new printing technologies with the rise of capitalism. Print-capitalism only succeeded when many people could read and write. The establishment of mass educational systems and the reduction of illiteracy helped extend new economic relations to larger societal sectors. Print-capitalism also provided incentives for the creation of grammars and dictionaries. In fact, after the Bible, dictionaries were the first books published in the fifteenth and sixteenth centuries (Rice and Grafton, 1994). Ironically, the democratization of reading during the Renaissance also brought about the systematic censorship of books, something rare during the Middle Ages (Rice and Grafton, 1994). Dictionaries and grammars helped disseminate the newly standardized and dominant languages through the educational systems. Print-capitalism produced the imagined communities that evolved into nations and nation-states. The choice of languages in education became political decisions that reflected the relative capability of competing ethnolinguistic groups to tie their language to the defining features of their nation-state. Modern public education systems, in turn, emerged as agencies that helped disseminate those languages and their values.

Education is also political because of its unmatched capacity for political socialization. It can make populations internalize norms, rules, and values. Children enter schools at a very young age and spend there many hours a day, several days a week, numerous weeks a year, and many years. All that time they are learning diverse information, concepts, skills, social norms, and values. When it comes to socializing a population, no other institution besides the family can come close. Educational systems, from the beginning, embodied the cosmologies of the ruling classes. They still do. It is no coincidence that virtually after every change in regime, either by revolution, *coup d'état* or elections, there is a restructuring of the educational system. Politicians know the power of education and use it.

Public educational systems also affect class cleavages, either by reinforcing the existing differences or ameliorating them. Since a good education is a fundamental asset to compete for good jobs, in those countries where access to the best schools is a privilege of the wealthy, the poor have few chances for upward social mobility. If decent public education is available for most people, it can increase the chances of the poor sectors to compete for lucrative jobs and improve social mobility.

Public education systems also created an important societal sector: the teachers. There appeared a large group of people sharing interests, playing a crucial role in society, and eventually organizing in unions. Certainly there were teachers before the emergence of nation-states, but never in the quantities and with the class consciousness of modern times. They tend to enjoy much prestige within their communities, which makes them potential political figures. In Puerto Rico, for example, public school teachers and state university professors who run for political office are allowed to take a paid leave of absence for the semester of the election. If they are elected, their job is reserved for them until they return.

Language and Politics

Diversity is the main reason for language's political nature. There are more than 6,000 live languages in the world. In Africa alone there are over 2,000 different languages. There are more than 700 languages spoken in Indonesia, over 400 in India, and around 800 in Papua-New Guinea (Lewis, 2009). Most European industrialized countries like Great Britain, Spain, Switzerland, Italy, France, Belgium, Sweden, and Norway have significant language minorities. Even in the Americas, dominated by five European tongues, there are more than 15 other languages spoken by at least one million people. Virtually no country in the world can claim linguistic homogeneity. Even Japan is facing language diversity, as evidenced by the policy of promoting the learning of Japanese among immigrants. The increasing migration of workers and refugees, provoked by the globalization of international markets and wars, has created linguistic minorities in places where there had been none before (Tollefson, 2002: 5). Hence, while the total number of differentiated languages is on the descent, language diversity worldwide is increasing.

Language heterogeneity produces an unbreakable nexus between language and politics. This link affects at least five general aspects of modern states: (1) national identity, (2) racial relations, (3) bureaucratic efficiency, (4) income distribution, and (5) political participation.

A language affects the national identity of a state when it is a component of the dominant group's distinctiveness. It becomes associated with the state at the expense of competing language groups (Tollefson, 2002; Solé, 1995). This association creates a tension that becomes manifested through political competition. This competition then creates a significant basis for ethnolinguistic tensions that are expressed in many ways, the most extreme form being armed conflict. For instance, the unification of the Spanish state in the fifteenth and sixteenth centuries not only established Castile's political and economic dominance, but also elevated its defining symbols to those of Spain, particularly the language (Laitin, Solé, and Kalyvas, 1994; Valleverdú, 1984). Spain's unity, however, remained uneasy with several conflicts revolving around the language status of Catalonia, the Basque Country, and Galicia. Conversely, a state may favor language diversity. It may foment divisions among language groups in order to neutralize a potentially unified opposition, like Yugoslavia before 1980 during the Tito regime (Tollefson, 2002:181).

The effects of language over racial relations are well illustrated with the resurgence of language discrimination in the U.S. Using language as a mask, "anglos are allowed to do and say all kinds of things without appearing overtly racist" (Zentella, 2003:53). Unlike race, language is something over which a person has control. It can be changed. If a person cannot speak the Standard English he can be stigmatized, mocked, and discriminated. That cannot happen with race, openly. But it happens. The groups that speak a different version of English or another language in the U.S. are precisely the racial minorities of the country: Latinos, African Americans, Native Americans, and Asians. Hence, racial discrimination hides behind the veil of language prejudice and promotes the same economic marginalization.

Language also impinges on a state's bureaucratic efficiency. Bureaucratic efficiency refers to the capacity of the state to perform administrative duties at the maximum level of utility. The existence of diverse language groups potentially reduces a state's bureaucratic efficiency by swelling the costs of official communication at central and regional levels. Official documents may have to be translated; public education may have to include several language courses or media of instruction; state offices may be forced to hire personnel speaking more than one language; translators may be needed for the legal system.

States may choose to operate in one language to control expenses, but it is likely to isolate population sectors or even entire regions. Language diversity may also disrupt the communications between the central government and some political units, or among political units. It has an effect on social mobilization—in Deutsch's terms, the process by which isolated sectors of the population are drawn into fuller participation in public life through the opening of centers of political control, economic power, and innovation in outlying areas (1961). The difficulty to communicate between the center and outlying areas raises real obstacles for the integration of those sectors into national life.

Language issues also affect income distribution. They influence differences in employment opportunities among language groups. Where many private enterprises require the use of a particular language, the population sectors that lack proficiency in that language become marginalized. Those possessing the language skills reap larger shares of the employment pie. In fact, language diversity may transform or reinforce class cleavages based on language proficiency differences. Québec, for instance, implemented a pro-French policy that helped to transform the distribution of riches in its society. English was, until 1969, the dominant language in the province's business community, which produced significant earning differentials between Francophones and Anglophones (Burnaby, 2002; Grin, 1996; Hamers and Hummel, 1994). Legislation in Québec's parliament since 1969 reversed that trend, imposing the use of French in the workplace. It quickly had a noticeable impact in reducing income gaps between Anglophones and Francophones. Language diversity can also contribute to income disparities through the use of various languages at different levels of production. For instance, one language may be used at shop levels and another at managerial positions. This is the situation of many Spanish-speaking factory workers in large U.S. cities, whose supervisors speak only English and establish communication through intermediate level supervisors that serve as interpreters. A similar case can be made for agricultural industries in states such as California, where a large number of low level jobs are occupied by Spanish-speaking Mexican and Central American immigrants while managerial level jobs are occupied by English-speaking individuals of Anglo-Saxon origin (Solé, 1995). The American case illustrates how language can provide a foundation for the permanence of class differentiations between ethnolinguistic groups (Bloom and Grenier, 1992:445–451). This explains the pervasiveness of militant language stakeholders in the United States, like the Official English Movement and the *Academia Norteamericana de la Lengua Española*.

Finally, language diversity may produce the exclusion from political affairs of individuals and population sectors who cannot communicate in the language or languages of the state. Parliamentary debates are held in one language or possibly two, but a plurality of languages would make communication hopeless in legislative discussions. Local, regional, state, or provincial legislatures and administrations may allow the use of other languages and permit some levels of participation by individuals who do not speak the state's language. This practice, however, hinders the national leaders' capacity to communicate with regional governments and population sectors that cannot speak the central language. Interpreters are often used, but the increase in costs and the additional efforts to communicate produce biases against the full inclusion of marginalized language groups in political decisions. Governments may also prevent ethnolinguistic groups from gaining access to government posts, which constitute a large sector of the job market in most countries. Rahman (1996) showed how Punjabi elites in Pakistan used Urdu and English to control a disproportionate fraction of the jobs in the public sector. Urdu, spoken by about 8 percent of the population, was required in most government jobs, at the expense of Punjabi, the mother tongue of over 48 percent of the Pakistani people. In Africa and Asia, French and Belgian colonial policies provided access to French training only to a handful of privileged people who could serve as native auxiliaries (Babault and Caitucoli, 1997:160). The rest of the population remained intentionally excluded from the political and economic advantages that the proficiency in the French language provided. In independent Senegal, French, spoken by a minority, was chosen as the official language of government while 90 percent of the population communicated in Wolof (Grosjean, 1982). Another instance is Haiti, where most people speak Creole but French dominates the official business of government.

Language Rationalization versus Language Diversity

The educational language policies of most countries draw a line between the social importance of many languages and their weight in public educational systems. The central dilemma that policymakers face when deciding the role of languages in education is whether to favor one or several languages. Policymakers traditionally perceive a tradeoff between inclusiveness and efficiency. Where a single language is favored, it does so at the expense of other languages. Where several languages are chosen, resources are drained. The problem can approach a zero-sum game when it comes to the effects over language communities. In many cases, as one linguistic group is helped by the relative emphasis on their language, another linguistic group is harmed. In any given school curriculum there is a finite number of languages that can be used in a significant manner. The win of one is, more or less, the loss of other or others. That makes these policies so potentially conflictive.

In the social realm, languages serve as systems of communication and as instruments of control. People communicate at various levels, with different people, and for diverse purposes. Hence, language social use is dynamic and has the potential to change. Sociolinguists have identified several social functions of language, including group use, wider communication, official use, and religious purposes (Stewart, 1968; Ferguson, 1966). All functions may not be fulfilled by the same language. For example, English may play an important public role in India, but a small part in home use (Parasher, 1980). In contrast, local languages hold important places for home use but are less relevant for the job market. Languages may also share a social function. Many countries, developing and industrialized, have adopted English as the language of employment in international business fields, with native languages preferred for domestic jobs. This book focuses on the language function that relates to wider communication, which can be measured by recoding population census data. Chapter 2 recodes census data in a way that reduces errors associated with the potential lack of precision of census information. The chapter also introduces a typology that categorizes languages within a continuum ranging from primary to foreign use. Categories are based on intensity of use, rather than on qualitative distinctions. The continuum is a way to solve the problem of rigidity in some of the language categories proposed in earlier works.

The use of a language in education can be placed in two general categories: (1) as media of instruction and (2) as language courses. School curricula often contain more than one language as media of instruction. Various courses may be taught in one language while others are taught in another language, or different grades may use different languages. Several languages may also be taught as course subjects within the same grades or at different levels. Chapter 2 develops indicators to quantify the educational use of a language based on whether it is a medium of instruction or a course subject, and for how long. The indicators for educational use produce values that are measured against a scale that fluctuates from primary to foreign use. Hence, the scales for language social use and language educational use have the same range so they can be compared across cases. The potential difference between both values shows the magnitude of the educational language gap (ELAG) for a given language within a particular country or region. ELAG represents an instrument to provide precise evidence of a language's relevance in one of modern society's main institutions: the school system.

The Politics of Educational Language Policies

The policymakers' dilemma between language rationalization and diversity uncovers the importance of political variables over considerations of language in education. The issue arises in (1) colonial relations, (2) challenges from national subunits, (3) demographic changes, (4) regime changes, (5) unfulfilled expectations, and (6) decisions over languages for international affairs.

The imposition of European languages in many African and Asian colonies during the nineteenth and twentieth centuries implied that languages which played no more than tertiary social roles were given primary uses in education to allow for colonial administration by Europeans and to train native cadres for colonial governance. Thus, English, French, Portuguese, Dutch, and Spanish obtained preferential roles in education, even though the overwhelming majorities of the colonies' populations could not speak them and had no social use for them. Another case was the imposition of English in the Philippines and Puerto Rico by the United States during the early twentieth century. This policy of *Americanization* attempted to raise the social role of English to that of a primary language through the use of the public school system.

Newly independent states with colonial histories often struggled to consolidate the incipient state institutions. One way to accomplish that was through the establishment of official languages. In Kenya, for instance, the Kenyatta administration made Swahili the national language, and English an official language. Public schooling began to use Swahili as a primary language for most of the population. The decision to favor Swahili in governmental and educational functions, even though it was spoken by only one of the many Kenyan ethnic groups, responded to the need to develop a sense of pride in the country's African roots, which decades of British colonialism had impaired. The English language was favored over the other Kenyan native languages because it provided a tool for state administrative efficiency and continuity with the existing bureaucracy. Also, ironically for many ethnolinguistic groups, the use of English was perceived as less of a menace than Swahili, since it did not favor any particular ethnic group over the others. The young Kenyan state lacked the resources to establish an educational language policy based on diversity, opting for efficiency. Throughout the years, as the state apparatus consolidated, the educational language policies shifted towards larger roles for minority languages.

Some national subunits, such as Québec, underwent significant language policy modifications without experiencing the type of regime changes produced by independence processes. The Québécois government approved a series of legislative pieces through the 1970s that substantially modified the role of French in education, at the workplace and in government. Québec increased its autonomy from the central Canadian government during the 1980s and consolidated its language policy.

The effects of demographic changes in language policies can be seen in the diverse experiences with bilingual education in the United States. Bilingual education programs use several languages but Spanish dominates because of the larger rate of growth of Hispanics in the United States (Tucker, 2005). Most bilingual education programs were adopted after intense pressure from organized political groups, whose numbers provided them with influence over public opinion and elections.

Other countries that traditionally ignored minority language rights, like Nicaragua, reviewed their policies after new increased demands sparkled by regime changes. English Creole speakers in Nicaragua took advantage of the participation spaces opened by the Sandinista government during the 1980s, and managed to secure bilingual education programs that had been inconceivable under the Somoza dictatorship. Conversely, Franco's Spain managed to suppress Catalan demands for language rights, but the democratic regime created by the 1978 constitution cleared the way for the inclusion of Catalan in education.

In India, the post-independence use of English as an official language was meant as a temporary policy, since Hindi was intended to remain the sole official language and the principal medium of instruction after several years of social and political adaptation. However, the identification of Hindi with a specific region of the country produced resentments from non-Hindi speaking regions, which preferred the use of the language of the British Empire over that of the dominant Indian state.

Languages of international use have existed since ancient times. Ancient Greek, Latin, Sanskrit, Arabic and Mandarin spread well beyond the boundaries of their respective ethnolinguistic groups. In modern times, imperial languages such as Spanish, French, Portuguese, Dutch, Russian, and English spread across geographical expanses at rates never experienced before. More recently, the era of globalization, with the preeminence of the United States, reinvigorated English as the preferred international language. Hence, over 50 countries have adopted educational language policies favoring English, even though most of them have no significant English speaking populations (Wright, 2004; Maurais and Morris, 2004). English is perceived as the language of trade and communication and consequently as an instrument of social mobility. Even the European Union, with its enormous economic and political clout, constantly debates over the unique stance of the English language. South Korea established in 1997 a school language program that made English instruction compulsory since the third grade. Slovenia, a model for the respect of linguistic human rights, inserted English courses in its elementary school curriculum (Tollefson, 2002). Simultaneously, however, in most of those countries emerged a reaction against English instruction based on the defense of national cultures against linguistic imperialism (Jung and Norton, 2002).

The cases mentioned above differ in many ways, but all show the importance of political variables over educational language policies. They also illustrate the potential conflicts between language groups and state institutions, and among language groups themselves.

Centralization, Participation, and Language Stakeholders

Debates over school decentralization in the United States developed in response to social pressures in the 1960s and 1970s that wanted to improve the quality of education and change the power relations in education (Wissler and Ortiz, 1986:280). Advocates of centralized systems generally argue that decentralization impairs the development of coherent and effective curricula, which shows in the poor performance of students from the decentralized American public school system, compared to those of other industrialized countries with more centralized educational structures (Clune, 1993; Smith and O'Day, 1990). Proponents of decentralization, on the other hand, claim that a dispersion of power among parents and teachers allows them to take responsibility and ownership over their schools' curricula, which in turn produces flexible policies that respond to particular communities' needs (Hammad and Norris, 2009; Gaziel, 2008; Hill, 1997; Kerchner and Koppich, 1993; Hannaway and Carnoy, 1993). Regardless of differences, most scholars agree that the levels at which educational policies are developed affect the outcomes.

Relative to language in education, variations in decisionmaking levels provide policymakers with different incentives and options to gather information and establish policies. Central levels of authority offer motivations to gather information about the language use in society as a whole rather than about small communities. Information gathering is expensive, and specialized information requires trained personnel and research resources, both of which are usually scarce in public school systems. Hence, educational governance structures with concentrations of power at the central level have incentives to favor language rationalization over language diversity.

Decisionmakers at low levels of authority, away from the center, tend to have more information about the particular communities affected by their decisions. Hence, for them, gathering information about language habits within their community is a relatively inexpensive operation. This, in turn, increases the likelihood of establishing educational language policies that reflect linguistic differences among various communities. Decentralized structures allow local boards to concentrate on more specific plans, geared toward communities' needs without having to incur in the kinds of costs that systemic plans demand.

The most relevant language stakeholders in the question of *who* makes policies are bureaucrats, teachers, parents, and nonsystem actors. Bureaucrats have strong incentives to seek states' language rationalizing policies, and institutional constraints against language diversity. Parents and teachers, who by virtue of their own experiences are aware of the specific social uses of languages in their communities, have incentives to seek educational language policies that reflect diversity.

Bureaucrats are government employees, and as such, respond to the rationalizing tendency of the state with a preference on a small number of languages for government use, the logic of which is based on efficiency. Administrators strive to manage their relatively scarce resources in an efficient manner, achieving the best results with the fewest expenses. Since several languages in an administrative structure increase the operational expenses, the bureaucratic perspective favors a reduction in languages used in education. The bureaucracy's perspective tends to favor rationalization over diversity. Thus, bureaucrats in education departments have historically favored prominent educational roles for languages that are widely used for government and business purposes, even if they had little social use otherwise.

Assessing teachers' interests is a complicated task since their participation can take many forms, from centralized unions to school councils, to individual actions. Unions focus on job security and wage issues, so language policies may play secondary roles to salary scales, tenure, and hiring practices. Participation of teachers at the lower levels of educational systems, where they are members of the communities, provide more incentives for accurate reflections of language social uses in schools than higher, more centralized levels of participation, where class motivations dominate community interests. Ultimately then, teachers' interests are strongly influenced by the level at which they participate.

Parents may have the largest stake in educational decisions since their children are the clients of school policies. As citizens, parents are aware of the social roles played by languages within their communities. As consumers of educational services, parental interests may be summarized in two general preferences. First, since language is so often a significant aspect of group identity, parents have a tendency to support a prominent educational status of their mother tongue. Second, parents want education to provide social mobility opportunities. Hence, parents also favor significant roles for languages that are used widely in government and business transactions. Since a school curriculum can accommodate several languages for diverse purposes, parents may support the intense use of more than one language. For instance, where a mother tongue is not widely used in businesses or government agencies, parents almost invariably favor some combined use of their mother tongue with a language considered valuable for employment.

Nonsystem actors may be as varied as societies themselves. They often involve political parties, particularly those with nationalist ideologies, such as the *Parti Québécois* in Canada or the *Partido Nacionalista Vasco* in Spain. Nonsystem actors also involve special interest groups, such as the Official English Movement in the United States. Their interests are diverse, and they can only be understood within their particular historic junctures.

Language stakeholders play a central role on this analysis. The book identifies the language stakeholders involved in several educational policies in Puerto Rico between 1898 and 2013 and explores their relative success. Language stakeholders in Puerto Rico include: (1) teachers unions (*Asociación de Maestros de Puerto Rico, Federación de Maestros de Puerto Rico*), (2) political parties (*Partido Unión, Partido Nuevo Progresista, Partido Popular Democrático, Partido Independentista Puertorriqueño*), (3) prominent individuals (José de Diego, Rubén del Rosario), (4) private organizations (*Ateneo de Puerto Rico, Academia Puertorriqueña de la Lengua Española*), and (5) government officials (Roland Falkner, Mariano Villaronga, Ramón Mellado). The main reason for the failure of the Americanization strategy between 1898 and 1948 was the lack of language stakeholders in favor who were able and willing to invest their time and resources into influencing the educational language policy. The U.S. occupation of

Puerto Rico in 1898 did not provoke a mass migration of Anglophones to the island, which in turn precluded the development of a large English linguistic community that perceived the maintenance of their language as fundamental for the group's survival. Ironically, most language stakeholders who defended the Americanization policies were not English native speakers. Some couldn't even speak it. Hence, English language stakeholders never reached a critical mass that would make it rational for most people to support an all-English curriculum (Laitin, 1993). Conversely, the defense of Spanish during the Americanization era and its promotion during the Puertoricanization policy of 1949 were backed by a wide coalition of language stakeholders, which Algrén (1987) called the "Movement against Teaching English," and Clampitt-Dunlap (2000) termed the "defenders of language." Eventually, the growth of the pro-statehood movement and the return migration during the 1970s of second generation Puerto Ricans from the U.S., whose native tongue was English, provided the ideology and the language stakeholders to break the consensus on the educational language policy of Puertoricanization and to reinvigorate the debate over the role of English in public schools. The public disputes over the attempted policy of English immersion during the late 1990s evidenced that there were relevant language stakeholders willing and able to pay the costs of influencing a pro-English language policy. The fact that the policy faced a fierce opposition from many pro-Spanish language stakeholders does not blur the fact that many people supported the immersion programs. Puerto Rico in 1996 was very different than in 1900, and the resulting policies reflected those differences.

Education departments with strong centralization and little participation tend to produce results that favor the interests of small elites often associated with the ruling class (see Figure 1.1). The educational language policies produced on these cases favor language rationalization over language diversity, in many cases imposing a language spoken by a minority. This was the case of Puerto Rico between 1898 and 1949.

Decentralized and participatory institutions, by contrast, offer incentives to establish educational language policies based on community needs with the inclusion of parents and teachers. Such is the case of Finland and Switzerland. The educational language policies in those cases favor diversity over rationalization, and often expressly protect linguistic human rights. Another possibility is to have a highly centralized system with a large degree of participation from societal sectors, like the French and Austrian school systems. This case promotes the existence of centralized and strong teachers unions, whose main weapons are their strength in numbers and their influence over educational policies. The resulting educational language policies are based on rationalization, but with relatively large spaces for diversity. Hence, the French system may appear intolerant against English interference, but flexible towards Corsican. The Austrians may protect their German against English, but not against Italian. Finally, a public school system may be decentralized but with small levels of participation. This was the experience of Japan during the American occupation after World War II, which allowed local kingpins to control the schools' operations without the communities' involvement. Language diversity seems to prevail over rationalization more often than otherwise.

Figure 1.1 Types of Decisionmaking in Educational Systems

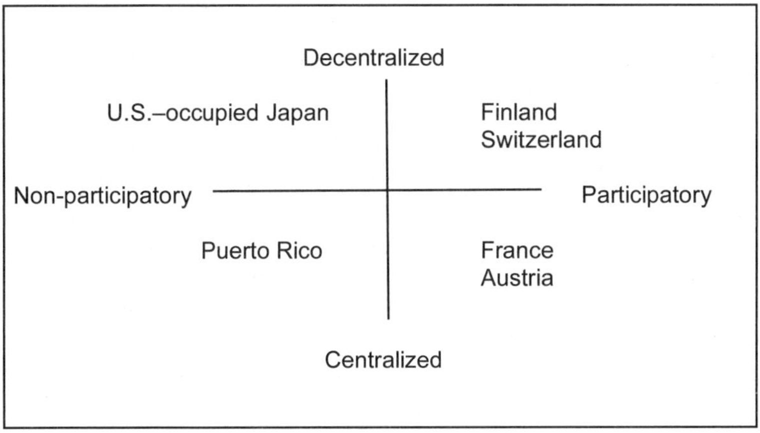

```
                        Decentralized
          U.S.–occupied Japan    |    Finland
                                 |    Switzerland
Non-participatory  ——————————————+—————————————— Participatory
                    Puerto Rico  |    France
                                 |    Austria
                         Centralized
```

A Nation as a Language Laboratory

The book covers several historical periods in the development of Puerto Rico's educational language policies. The time periods considered here offer general theoretical insights and a better understanding of Puerto Rico's history, divided in three policy eras. The first period corresponds to the Americanization era, which lasted from 1898 to 1948. The second period, the Puertoricanization era, extended from 1949 to 1968. The last is the Bilingualization era, from 1969 to the present.

The case studies' theoretical contributions are three-fold. First, they provide evidence of the importance of domestic variables in comparative politics. If international variables alone could contain the whole story, Puerto Rico would be an ideal case for it, due to the imposing presence of U.S. political, military and economic dominance. However, as will be seen in this book, in the evolution of the island's language policies, domestic variables played a role at least equally important as the colonial institutions and actors. Second, the Puerto Rican case shows the effects of institutional changes on public policies. The incipient education department of Puerto Rico in 1900 suffered several changes through the periods considered in the study, and those changes were accompanied almost immediately by modifications in educational language policies. In fact, each one of the three educational policy eras in Puerto Rico was preceded by a significant change in the education department. Third, an understanding of the development of educational language policies in Puerto Rico may establish the bases for similar studies in other countries where language policies in education also create political tensions. Thus, the study of cases like Aruba, Québec, Catalonia, India and Nigeria should benefit from insights developed through the exploration of Puerto Rico's educational institutions.

The book's empirical observations also contribute to the knowledge of Puerto Rican politics through the analysis of many changes in government institutions and educational structures. In doing so, the book provides a systematic examination of the school system's development in terms of decisionmaking locus and actors' involvement in policymaking. Since this aspect of the Puerto Rican educational system has not been studied before from a political scientific perspective, this study opens new ground. This book also stresses the domestic policymakers' choices, and shifts the focus of explanatory variables from Washington to Puerto Rico, which few explanations of the Americanization strategy do (López Yustos, 1997; Morris, 1995; Solís, 1994; Negrón de Montilla, 1990; Cebollero, 1945).

Methodological Considerations

The empirical analysis of this project centers on various language policy developments in Puerto Rico for over 100 years. The empirical focus is in one country, but the theoretical framework was developed from the scrutiny of an ample literature covering a wide array of experiences from different regions and countries (San Román, 2013; Iannàccaro and Dell'Aquila, 2011; Moravcsik, 2007; Tucker, 2005; Maurais and Morris, 2004; Wright, 2004; Torres González, 2002; Barreto, 2001; Laitin, 1998, 1992, 1977; Babault and Caitucoli, 1997; Rahman, 1996; Solé, 1995; Morris, 1995; Hamers and Hummel, 1994; Crawford, 1992;

Rodino, 1992; Anderson, 1990; Eastman, 1990; Negrón de Montilla, 1990; Esteva i Fabregat, 1984; Sabater, 1984; Dutcher, 1982; Parasher, 1980; Kuo, 1979). The use of one case illustrates a theoretical approach intended to apply in most countries where language diversity poses challenges to educational policies. In this sense, the selection of Puerto Rico serves as a means to perform a plausibility probe (King, Keohane, and Verba, 1994:209).

Puerto Rico, as a Caribbean nation, belongs to a region with many different linguistic experiences. For instance, Haiti expanded the role of Creole in education, where it had practically no presence before, which is a puzzling policy for the poorest country of the Western Hemisphere, since Haitian Creole has no function in international markets. Haiti exists in contrast with its neighbor, Jamaica, where English Creole has received little attention from official educational policies. Caribbean experiences with language policies are as diverse as the islands themselves, and the region displays a unique language kaleidoscope, including French, Spanish, English, Dutch, Creole (Haitian and Jamaican), Patois (French, Dutch, and English), Hindi, and Papiamento. The picture becomes even more complex if continental countries around the Caribbean basin are included (Venezuela, Suriname, Guyana, French Guyana, Colombia, Panama, Belize, Nicaragua, Costa Rica, Honduras, and Mexico), with languages such as Sranang Tongo, Hindustani, Gaifuna, Maya and Nahuatl. Hence, the Caribbean represents a relatively untapped source of validation for several theoretical tenets regarding the development of educational language policies.

Caribbean language policies have received the attention of several scholars (Hebblethwaite, 2012; St. Hilaire, 2009; Brown-Blake, 2008; Bobonis and Toro, 2007; Pousada, 2006; Clampitt-Dunlap, 2000; Robertson, 1990). However, most of the attention has focused on areas with larger populations like North America (Subtirelu, 2013; De Korne, 2010; Mady and Turnbull, 2010; Bourhis, 1994; Fortier, 1994; Hamers and Hummel, 1994; Laponce, 1987; Meadwell, 1993), Europe (San Román, 2013; Moreno-Fernandez, 2008; Huguet, 2006), West Africa (Wyrod, 2008; Bangura, 2000), and East Asia (Hornberger and Vaish, 2009). But, in spite of the small size of most islands and their small population, Caribbean cases can provide insights into other regions' experiences for several reasons. First, the archipelago encompasses a wide range of political arrangements, including longstanding sovereign states (Haiti, Dominican Republic, Cuba), independent states (Jamaica, Trinidad and Tobago, the Bahamas), overseas departments (French Guyana, Guadeloupe, Martinique), dependencies (Bermuda, Curaçao, St. Maarten, Aruba), and unincorporated territories (U.S. Virgin Islands,

Puerto Rico). Second, the Caribbean region contains important differences in linguistic homogeneity. Some countries are fairly homogeneous, like Cuba, while others have competing linguistic groups, such as Trinidad and Tobago, Aruba, and Curaçao. Political and linguistic diversity are traits shared by most regions of the world, so conclusions from Caribbean experiences are likely to be useful in understanding universal language policy challenges.

Besides being part of the Caribbean region, Puerto Rico bears several peculiarities that make it useful for this study. First, since the end of the Spanish-Cuban-American War of 1898, the island has been spared from the kinds of revolutionary moments and sudden breaks with the past so common in Latin American history. Hence, political institutions have evolved gradually since the civilian government was established in 1900 and policy changes believed to be caused by institutional developments can be observed without having to consider extraordinary circumstances. Second, while Puerto Rico's population is overwhelmingly Spanish-speaking, English plays a major role in education due to political reasons (allegiance to the United States) and economic considerations (social mobility). Hence, the Spanish-speaking majority of Puerto Rico contends with issues that often affect language minorities in other countries. Third, Puerto Rico maintains an uneasy political relationship with the United States, mainly because of ethnic differences, which echoes other unresolved political relationships, like Québec with Canada and Catalonia with Spain. Since language is, in all three examples, among the critical sources of political tensions, understanding language policy decisions in one place can provide insights into larger issues of nationalism and political integration elsewhere.

Book Plan

The book is divided in seven chapters. Chapter 1 summarizes the objectives, discusses the intersection of politics and linguistics, and explains the theoretical foundations. Chapter 2 provides an instrument to measure the language social use, the language educational use, and the educational language gap (ELAG). Chapter 3 discusses the preferences over language educational policies by language stakeholders: teachers, administrators, parents, students, and nonsystem actors. It presumes a rational process of decisionmaking, but limited by the institutional features of the educational system. Chapter 4 analyses the three major paradigms in educational language policies in Puerto Rico since 1898: Americanization, Puertoricanization, and Bilingualization. The discussion of each period includes the major features of the policies and the changes within them. Chapter 5 produces indexes for the historical use of English in the social and educational realms in Puerto Rico from 1898 to 2013. The chapter also includes an analysis of the changes in ELAG for the same period. It shows that English social use began as a tertiary language in 1898 and gradually grew into its current status as a secondary language with primary elements. In turn, the educational use of English moved from a primary language to a tertiary language with secondary elements. Chapter 6 describes the preferences and actions of the language stakeholders in Puerto Rico. Among them are teachers unions, education commissioners, political parties, parents, and students. Chapter 7 establishes how the book's objectives were met, discusses the main contributions and suggests additional research questions.

2

The Educational Language Gap

Languages perform several functions within a given society, such as education, wider communication, religious interactions, inter and intra group communication, economic relations, and international affairs. Most ethnolinguistic groups that seek governmental support sustain their claims on the basis that their language serves some degree of wider communication, or social use. From this perspective, a state that does not protect a language with a significant social use is considered unfair. This is especially true in cases where a language plays an important role of wider communication but has a limited presence in the educational system. Given the importance of literacy and education for the existence of a language, a disparity between the language's use for wider communication and its use in education may represent the difference between survival and extinction. Linguistic groups typically demand that their language should be included in the school curriculum and used as a medium of instruction. Advocates of linguistic human rights may expect the social role of a language in a given polity to have a corresponding presence on the school system, particularly in public education. However, the empirical evidence suggests that in most cases minority languages are underrepresented in their countries' public school systems, while dominant languages are overrepresented. The concept of educational language gap provides an instrument to measure precisely the relationship between a given language's social and educational uses.

Language Social Use

Ferguson's 1959 paradigmatic article, "Diglossia," established one of the foundations for understanding the social roles of languages and created a line of research that still inspires countless scholars around the world.[1] Diglossia described the situation in which two varieties of one language served precise and distinct purposes, where a High (H) variety was more prestigious and used in formal occasions while a Low (L) variety was less prestigious and used in informal settings. The empirical application of the concept concentrated on four diglossic circumstances: (1) French and Creole in Haiti, (2) Classical and Egyptian Arabic in Egypt, (3) Standard and Swiss German in Switzerland, and (4) Classical and Modern Greek in Greece. In a latter piece, Ferguson (1966) described seven social functions of a language, where diglossia embodied a particular distribution of those functions. For instance, High languages performed the functions of official use, educational use, and international use, while Low languages satisfied the functions of group and intergroup communications (Ferguson, 1966; Fasold, 1987:63). Ferguson (1959:331) also established a link between language use and acquisition, stating that "L tends to be learned at home as a mother tongue..., (while) the learning of H is accomplished by the means of formal education."

Another major theoretical step in the understanding of languages' social roles was the introduction of the concept of "verbal repertoires," which referred to the "totality of linguistic forms regularly used in the course of socially significant interaction" (Gumperz, 1964:138). Gumperz claimed that people played diverse social roles and used particular linguistic forms according to those roles. For example, the same individual could be a mother, a wife, a factory worker, a friend and a religious follower. She may engage a conversation with a friend in a casual language variety, while recurring to a formal version when relating to coworkers or fellow religious worshipers. According to Gumperz, individuals pick the appropriate linguistic form according to two social functions: transactional and personal. The transactional function applied to "limited socially defined goals" (1964:149), like religious services and official government operations. The personal function of a language pertained to informal situations, such as among friends and peer groups. Gumperz did not refer to the term "diglossia" and avoided the hierarchical terminology associated with it, but his description of the transactional and personal functions was very similar to Ferguson's portrayal of the settings where High and Low languages were used (Fasold, 1987:58).

Fishman (1967) applied the notion of diglossia to the social uses of different languages altogether. He identified distinct diglossic relationships between languages with no linguistic affinities, such as Spanish (High) and Guaraní (Low) in Paraguay. The concept evolved into "triglossia" (Mkilifi, 1978) and "polyglossia" (Platt, 1977). Fasold (1987) referred to "classic diglossia" as a way to depict the relationship between different versions of the same language, and to "superposed bilingualism" to describe the roles of distinct languages.

Laitin (1992) expanded on Gumperz's (1964) notion of "verbal repertoires" and Fasold's (1987) concept of "linguistic repertoires" to develop the idea of "language repertoires," which referred to the amount of languages an individual must use to participate in a country's realm of social mobility opportunities. Languages may occupy different social spaces, but those spaces could be fluid and overlapping (Laitin, 1992:5). Hence, contrary to the classical diglossia argument, several languages might share a social space, such as political meetings, government communications, or home use.

The concept of social function provided a framework for categorizing languages according to their relevance in a given society. Ferguson (1966) described three general language categories according to the function it played and the status it maintained. A *major language* serves the wider communication function (spoken by more than 25 percent of the population), has an official use, or is the medium of instruction of at least 50 percent of those completing secondary education (Ferguson, 1966:310). A *minor language* serves the group function (spoken by at least 5 percent of the population or by more than 100,000 people), or is used as the medium of instruction above the first years of primary instruction. A *language of special status* serves the religious function or international use.

Stewart (1968) developed the notion forward with a fluid categorization of languages, based on the function of wider communication and measured in terms of the percentage of speakers. A *class 1* language was one spoken by at least 75 percent of the population, a *class 2* by 50 percent, a *class 3* by 25 percent, a *class 4* by 10 percent, a *class 5* by 5 percent, and a *class 6* by less than 5 percent. These categories improved Ferguson's typology in that they accounted for more differences in degree than Ferguson's Major/Minor/Special Status qualitative categories.

I present a typology of six language categories that builds on Ferguson's and Stewart's strengths, and adds the dimension of the language official status, given the importance that government activities have over most citizens' lives. The typology combines quantitative census data (percentage of speakers) with qualitative data (official status). Table 2.1 provides the instrument to measure the relative social use of a language in a given state. The instrument is an adaptation of a methodology used by economists to measure the independence of a central bank, in which researchers identify several criteria that measure "a few narrow but relatively precise legal characteristics" (Cukierman, et al, 1992:356). Variables receive weights and codes according to theoretical assumptions but recognizing that the measurement of central bank independence is "difficult and inevitably requires subjective judgment" (Cukierman, et al, 1992: 356). My model also measures a few narrow and precise variables, recognizing that there is an element of subjectivity defined by the theoretical assumptions presented in the book.

Table 2.2 takes the values produced by Table 2.1 and classifies them in six language categories: (1) primary, (2) secondary with primary elements, (3) secondary, (4) tertiary with secondary elements, (5) tertiary, and (6) foreign.

A primary language is that which dominates the linguistic spectrum in a given society even if it shares significant portions with other languages. A secondary language with primary elements is that which plays a significant, but not predominant role. It is a minority language that shares aspects of a primary language. For instance, it may be an official language or a social mobility tool. It may be the preferred choice in school for second-language teaching for nonnative speakers. A secondary language with primary elements may also be in a growing process that may provoke it to challenge the existing primary language for political space. A secondary language plays a relevant but more moderate role. It may be a regional or religious language. Also, its speakers represent less than half the total population. A tertiary language with secondary elements is a minor language that plays a disproportionately large role due to regional concentration, legal status, economic relevance, religious ceremonies, or colonial relations. A tertiary language is that which occupies a very minimal but consistent space in a given society. These may be small immigrant settlements or small economic interests. A foreign language is one that plays no role in a society.

The inclusion of intermediate categories, such as tertiary with secondary elements, adds dynamism to the traditional classifications. They account for the blurry areas where two types overlap. For instance, when does a language cease to be a widely used second language and becomes a primary language? When does a foreign language assume a relevant role and becomes a second language? Those intermediate categories allow us to identify the stage when a language is in a transition to a qualitatively different category.

Coding the census information according to wide categories reduces the effects of the potential inaccuracies in information gathering by census data described earlier. For instance, a language reported to be used by 81 percent of the population in a state where it is one of two official languages receives a value of 0.87, which corresponds to that of a primary language. Had there been a measurement error in the census data, say 3 percent, the value would have remained within the same category and received a similar coding. Coding data information does not eliminate potential errors, but reduces their effects on the language classification.

Table 2.1 Language Social Use

Indicator	Weight	Coding
I. Segment of population that can speak the language	0.90	
90% to 100%		1.00
80% to 90%		0.88
60% to 80%		0.75
40% to 60%		0.63
20% to 40%		0.50
10% to 20%		0.38
5% to 10%		0.25
1% to 5%		0.13
0% to 1%		0.00
II. Official status	0.10	
Sole official or de facto national language		1.00
One of several official or de facto national languages; associate language		0.80
Official second language		0.60
Official regional language		0.40
Language of specific official ceremonies (such as crowning)		0.20
Language not among official languages		0.00

Table 2.2 Categories of Language Social Use

Language Class	Value
Primary	0.76 – 1.00
Secondary with Primary Elements	0.51 – 0.75
Secondary	0.26 – 0.50
Tertiary with Secondary Elements	0.16 – 0.25
Tertiary	0.06 – 0.15
Foreign	0.00 – 0.05

Educational Language Use

The classic literature on sociolinguistics contends that the High varieties of languages are almost always used for educational purposes (Ferguson, 1959). Languages used in education are standardized and possess written forms, grammars, dictionaries, and a minimal level of literary tradition. Low varieties often lack one or all of all those prerequisites, so their use in education is difficult. Moreover, the low status and limited use for social mobility reduced the incentives for policymakers to include them in the school curriculum. This is also the case where the diglossia happens among different languages, since many Low languages are often minority languages that do not have a literary tradition or even a written form. Those that have them often are not seen as agents of social mobility because they are not used for functions that provide jobs. However, the second half of the twentieth century experienced a steady awareness and growth in linguistic human rights demands from subjugated ethnolinguistic groups (Skutnabb-Kangas, 2006; Del Valle, 2003). Those demands have produced concrete gains in international law, like the United Nations Declaration of Language Rights (Hastings, 1997), labor laws, like Quebec's Bill 101, and pluralist educational policies (Paulston and Heidemann, 2006; May, 2006; Ricento, 1997). The school has come to represent an important arena for language maintenance and a concrete way to protect linguistic human rights. Implicit in most policy demands is the assumption that children need to be educated in their native language, often termed L1. The preeminence of L1 has been pointed out even in the learning of a second language. Hence, the educational use of a language, particularly the medium of instruction, is almost invariably one of the elements of most language policy debates.

Table 2.3 Educational Language Use

Indicator	Weight	Coding
I. Language as medium of instruction:	0.90	
Medium of instruction for ½ or more classes in all grades		1.00
Medium of instruction for ½ or more classes from 2nd or 3rd grade		0.88
Medium of instruction for ¼ to ½ of all courses from 1st, 2nd or 3rd grade		0.75
Medium of instruction for ½ or more classes from 4th, 5th or 6th grade		0.63
Medium of instruction for ¼ to ½ of all courses from 4th, 5th or 6th grade		0.50
Medium of instruction for ½ or more classes from 7th grade		0.38
Medium of instruction for ¼ to ½ of all courses from 7th grade		0.25
Medium of instruction for less than ¼ of all classes		0.13
No role as medium of instruction		0.00
II. Number of years taught:	0.10	
All school (1–12)		1.00
10 to 11 (2,3–12)		0.80
7 to 9 (4,5,6–12)		0.60
4 to 6 (7,8,9–12)		0.40
1 to 3 (10,11,12–12)		0.20
0		0.00

The literature on language learning typifies languages in education as native languages, second languages, foreign languages, heritage languages, and lingua francas (Cogo, 2012; Cook, 1999; Ortega, 2011; Tucker, 2005; Seidlhofer, 2004). The categories mix qualitative and quantitative criteria, and imply different teaching methodologies (Richards and Rodgers, 2001). For instance, the language teaching techniques for a native speaker presume competency, most commonly developed during childhood (Cruz-Ferreira, 2011:78). A second language approach aims at providing the students with enough knowledge to communicate with native speakers (Mitchel and Myles, 2004; Canale and Swain, 1980). It assumes there is little or no knowledge of the language by the learners, but some level of exposure to it outside the classroom. This approach is typical of minority language groups that learn a dominant language. The foreign language methodology is aimed at students that have no knowledge and little contact with the language. English, the current international lingua franca, is taught as a foreign language in many countries, whose students rarely use it in daily interactions but who expect it to provide them with a marketable skill in specialized jobs. Some scholars prefer the term "Teaching English as a Lingua Franca" to distinguish it from "Teaching English as a Foreign Language" (Seidlhofer, 2004; Dewey, 2007).

Table 2.4 Categories of Educational Language Use

Language Class	Value
Primary	0.76 – 1.00
Secondary with Primary Elements	0.51 – 0.75
Secondary	0.26 – 0.50
Tertiary with Secondary Elements	0.16 – 0.25
Tertiary	0.06 – 0.15
Foreign	0.00 – 0.05

This book presents six categories for the educational use of a language, which are similar to those of social use: (1) primary, (2) secondary with primary elements, (3) secondary, (4) tertiary with secondary elements, (5) tertiary, and (6) foreign. Indicators to measure the place of a language in education are based on two factors (Table

2.3). First is the use of the language as a medium of instruction. The second indicator is the number of years the language is taught as a subject. The more time is devoted to teaching a language, the closer it is to be treated as primary. Each indicator produces a value oscillating from 0 to 1, with a weight each of 0.90 and 0.10. The sum of both indicators generates a value fluctuating from 0 to 1, which is placed in a scale described in Table 2.4.

Educational Language Gap (ELAG)

One way to observe the effects of politics on education is through the comparison of language social and educational uses. If language use in the classroom were determined solely by the language's social use, values for language social use and educational language use should be equal or close to equal in most cases. But, since educational language uses in many countries differ greatly from language social use, and since decisions on educational language policies are political by nature, the difference between language *social* use and language *educational* use must be explained, at least in part, by political considerations.

The distance between the social and the educational uses of a language will be represented here in the form of a numerical variable labeled the "educational language gap," or ELAG. It measures how well the educational position of a language matches its social situation. ELAG is determined by the subtraction of language social use (Table 2.1) from educational language use (Table 2.3). For arguments' sake we may think of a case where the social use of a language scores a 0.87 while its educational value is 0.19. The scores mean that it occupies a social function of a primary language while it performs the educational function of a tertiary language with secondary elements. The value of ELAG, -0.68 (0.19 - 0.87), tells us that there is a large discrepancy between both uses of that particular language, and the minus sign indicates that it is underused in education. Another hypothetical language with a social use score of 0.09 and an educational use value of 0.78 tells us that it is being taught as a primary language while its social use barely reaches that of a tertiary language. The ELAG value of 0.69 shows that the language is overused in education. The reasons for the particular discrepancies are varied and context dependent, and there is no universal value judgment about whether it is a good or bad thing. However, in most cases, a language with a large social use but a small educational use, which produces a large and negative value for ELAG, shows a discrimination against a relatively large linguistic group. In other instances however, a large positive ELAG may reflect the case of an endangered language with little social use that is overemphasized in education because of its human, cultural, historical, religious, scientific or nationalistic value.

ELAG will provide us with a numerical representation of the conceptual difference between the social and educational uses of language. ELAG allows us to draw comparisons across cases and to establish correlations with other variables that may explain its changes, such as institutional decentralization and participation. Since the values of language social use and educational language use range from 0 to 1, ELAG has a minimum value of -1 and a maximum value of 1. As ELAG approaches 0 in either direction, the educational language policy is understood to better reflect the social use of that language. A positive value for ELAG implies a more intense use of a language in education than its social use, while a negative value means that its social use is higher than its educational use.

Changes in ELAG throughout time may mean one of two things. First, they may reflect changes in educational language policies, either towards or away from language social use. In both cases, political variables should be helpful in understanding the dynamics of policy formation that affected the change in educational language policies. Second, a change in ELAG may mean that there has been a change in language social use. Since patterns of language use evolve slowly, it is unlikely to find swift and large variations in ELAG based on changes in language social use. However, aggressive educational language policies aimed at changing language habits may, over time, prove effective. For instance, the initial period of a policy imposing a colonial language as the medium of instruction in schools would most likely show a large value for ELAG, since the colonial language would have a minimal social presence but an important role in education. Throughout time, ELAG's value may decrease if language policies were effective in developing a stronger social presence for the colonial language, thereby bridging the gap between language social use and educational language approach. Immigration in large numbers may also affect rapidly the social use of a language. One unforeseen effect of globalization has been the large migrations of people from developing countries into industrialized states, creating new ethnolinguistic minorities. Thus, explanations based on ELAG must be placed in context according to specific situations.

---

[1]For instance, the prestigious *International Journal of the Sociology of Language* dedicated one whole issue to the legacy of the concept (IJSL, 157, 2002).

3
Who's in Charge?

The literature on educational language policies, according to several leading sociolinguists, has emphasized the effects of language policies but overlooked the political processes and ideologies that produced those policies (Tollefson, 2002; Pennycook, 1997). As Tollefson (2002:6) argued, "the local dynamics of sociopolitical relations among competing ethnolinguistic groups must be carefully analyzed if the relationship between language and power is to be understood in a particular setting." The setting analyzed here is the educational system. The active participants in the dynamics of the sociopolitical relations among competing groups are the language stakeholders.

In order to understand the formulation of educational language policies, it is crucial to evaluate the groups involved in those determinations, the language stakeholders. All states confront the challenges of establishing language policies in education. Some are more conflictive than others, but they all share the existence of groups that attempt to translate their preferences into policies. After examining an extensive amount of cases around the world and through history, a number of similarities become evident. First, several groups appear constantly in policy debates, specifically teachers, parents, administrators, civil society groups, and political parties. Second, those groups express similar preferences across cases, even after controlling for their differences in culture, political systems, and socioeconomic development. Language stakeholders face parallel challenges in places like India (Sonntag, 2002; Das Gupta, 1998), South Africa (Smit, 1997), Puerto Rico (Torres González, 2002; Barreto, 2001), the United States (Wiley, 2002), Spain (Mar-Molinero, 2000), the Philippines (Bauzon, 1991; Benton, 1991), Yugoslavia (Tollefson, 2002), Hong Kong (Pennycook, 2002), and Paraguay (Mar-Molinero, 2000).

The study of Educational Language Policies (ELP) also needs to examine the political and educational institutions where the preferences of the language stakeholders meet. The nature of central educational ministries, provincial or regional bureaus, county agencies, local or community school boards, and schools affect the possibilities that those preferences may become policies and even mold the preferences themselves. For instance, centralized educational systems tend to promote the formation of national teachers' unions, which in turn are inclined to favor rationalization language policies over diversity. On the other hand, decentralized educational systems provide incentives for decentralized teachers' unions, which in turn tend to favor diversity over rationalization.

Educational Structures, Actors, and Preferences

The literature on educational policies is vast and covers a wide range of academic disciplines. Scholars have shown how educational policy studies have been enriched by contributions from various fields, including political science, psychology, sociology, anthropology, organizational studies, economics, and philosophy (Hornberger, 2003; Wong, 1994; Hannaway and Lockheed, 1986). The literature also covers an array of topics, such as curriculum development, educational finances, educational governance and management, teacher hiring and training, and student performance (Mehta, 2013; Craddock et al, 2013; Rata, 2012; Donato and Tucker, 2007; Hill, 1997; Lauglo, 1995; Clune, 1993; Hannaway and Carnoy, 1993; Wissler and Ortiz, 1986). Lauglo (1995) summarized the debates around two main themes: the distribution of authority, and the evaluation of quality and efficiency. This book addresses the former.

The distribution of authority within an educational system is essentially an issue of power allocation among actors (Hammad and Norris, 2009). Since the various actors have different and sometimes conflicting preferences, the relative power allocation within educational systems affects which preferences dominate, and, consequently, the types of policies established (Mavrogordato, 2012). Hence, one way to explain and predict educational policies in general and educational language policies in particular, is through the observation of changes in power distribution in the school system. This argument does not deny that pedagogical considerations are intrinsic to policy decisions, but rather that political concerns are at least equally relevant and have strong and independent effects on policy outcomes. This tenet, put forth by the field of critical applied linguistics, gained momentum among main stream sociolinguists (Schmidt, 2006; Tollefson, 2002; Pennycook, 1997).

Patterns of power distribution in schools systems can be observed in two ways: *where* they are created and *who* devises them. The issue of where policies are created refers to the various levels of decisionmaking: central educational ministry, regional or state body, school district, or individual school (Honig, 2004). The closer decisions are made to the central authority, the more centralized is the system. The opposite is true for decentralized systems. Large part of the literature on the debate over school reform, with a normative bias against centralization, assumes that decentralization increases the participation of non-bureaucratic actors (Castillo and Piñero, 2006; Beadie, 1996; Lauglo, 1995; Hannaway and Carnoy, 1993; Clune, 1993). This assumption stems from overlooking the distinction between participation and decisionmaking level. Decentralized systems may be more participatory in the sense of allowing lower hierarchical levels to take part in decisionmaking, but they may not be inclusive to groups outside the bureaucratic echelons. Vexliard (1970:44) showed how the American authorities during their occupation of Japan imposed decentralizing measures in the educational system that allowed reactionary and antidemocratic local authorities to seize control of many school districts. In this case, decentralization reduced democratic participation. In contrast, centralized educational systems may be inclusive and allow the involvement of teachers in important decisions. In such instances, many groups that traditionally demand greater participation may prefer a centralized system. National teachers' unions face strong incentives to claim their inclusion in decisionmaking at central levels, where their power in numbers is large, rather than to participate in decentralized, smaller units, where their strength may be reduced and where central union leaders may be less influential. It is no coincidence that in 1995 the *Asociación de Maestros de Puerto Rico* and the *Federación de Maestros de Puerto Rico*, rejected a government decentralization plan that proposed the creation of "community schools." One of their main concerns was the disenfranchisement of the unions by proposals to allow the hiring of teachers at school levels, which they believed curbed their influence and mobilization capacity, and jeopardized the status of teachers as state employees. Decentralization and participation are two distinct features of educational systems with independent effects on policy outcomes.

The other angle of the power distribution in educational systems is *who* devises educational policies. They can be grouped in two categories: *system actors* and *nonsystem actors*. System actors are those involved directly in educational policy, such as administrators and teachers. Nonsystem actors are those involved in domestic politics, usually politicians, political parties, organized social sectors, reform organizations, and universities (Coburn, 2005:23). Each group brings a particular and unique perspective to the educational process, which is reflected in their preferences on school policies. Those preferences meet on institutional arenas that refract the different interests. Institutions provide incentives and constraints that, in turn influence the language stakeholders' choices. The following section turns to a review of the stakeholders' preferences and the institutional constraints and incentives that modify them.

Administrators, Teachers, Parents, and Nonsystem Actors

In order to understand the policy effects of power allocation patterns in educational systems I will examine the language stakeholders involved in the decisionmaking process and their preferences regarding educational language use. Those preferences do not exist in vacuums, so they are affected by the administrative levels at which language policies are determined, and by their relative capacity to participate in educational policymaking.

Administrators

School administrators are bureaucrats at various levels of educational systems. Administrators include school principals, district superintendents, and central office executives. It is not a homogeneous group since it includes individuals involved in decisionmaking at different levels, facing diverse challenges and pressures. They have, however, important similarities in interests, preferences, and expectations.

Administrators face pressures from above and below, regardless of the level at which they operate. School principals receive claims from teachers and superintendents; superintendents encounter demands from principals, school boards and central offices; central offices confront challenges from teachers' unions, government officials, legislators, and the public opinion (Greenfield, 1995; Boyan, 1988a). Administrators are pivotal ingredients in the negotiated social order that is the school system (Cuchiara and Horvat, 2009: Gaziel, 2008; Greenfield, 1995; Bacharach and Mundell, 1993; Corwin and Borman, 1988), and are ultimately held responsible for the school system's performance. The nature of their posts makes them vulnerable to the particular groups that place demands on them, and, since different levels of administration face claims from different groups, the institutional effects on administrators' preferences vary according to the level of administration.

Their posts also force them to delegate important responsibilities, particularly to teachers. There is no absolute centralized and non-participatory educational system, since administrators have no choice but to delegate crucial tasks such as daily classroom operations to teachers. This delegation of responsibilities forces the administrators to rely on their teachers and contributes to the negotiated nature of school operations.

One of the main interests of administrators is efficiency (Marshall, 1991). Public school systems are almost invariably underfunded, which is a consequence of the attempt to educate large populations. Thus, administrators must care for numerous needs with limited budgets, and short-term, inexpensive, and productive programs tend to be favored over long-term, expensive and inefficient programs.

Besides efficiency, administrators seek stability and avoid crises among the many demands from the groups involved in educational processes (Honig, 2004; Greenfield, 1995; Corwin and Borman, 1988). School administrators are ultimately held accountable for the performance of schools, so the value of policy changes tends to be weighted against their potential destabilizing effects. Hence, administrators may favor change and innovation, but only if they do not threaten the precarious negotiated order of school operations. In an empirical study of several schools in the United States that experimented with shared decisionmaking, Weiss (1993) found that most of the drive for innovation came from school principals, rather than teachers. Weiss attributed this drive to the administrators' access to resources, their opportunity to communicate with wide sectors of the schools system, and their authority to bring the proposals to the attention of the school community (1993:83). However, the study also found that most changes focused on increasing the community's involvement in teaching activities, but few challenged the administrators' monopoly over school operations. Changes in classroom activities impacted the teaching aspects of schools' operations, but not the hierarchical rigidity that made administrators the sole overseers of schools' performance. Another empirical study compared the attempts by two principals to establish school governance reforms at different times in an inner city school in the southeastern United States (Bryant, 1998). While both implemented similar changes, they faced different structural constraints and incentives that allowed one to succeed and forced the other to fail. The failed attempt, according to Bryant, was doomed by the principal's incapacity to maintain a stable leadership role within the school community. When the reforms threatened the principal's leadership role, the principal's actions became conservative and stopped reform. In the successful case, in which the school principal was able to promote school reforms without jeopardizing his leadership position, he became an agent for change. More empirical research is still needed to draw conclusions about administrators' preferences toward school reforms, but the findings (Weiss and Bryant, 1998) provide strong support for the assumption that administrators may encourage change, but not at the expense of the stability of the school negotiated order.

The administrators' general inclinations on language policies are closely linked to their preferences for efficiency and stability. The use of various languages in education per se, needs not run against the administrators' preferences. However, their potential detrimental effects on efficiency and stability tend to provide incentives for administrators to prefer the use of the fewer languages possible. Language diversity challenges the state's administrative efficiency. In education, the use of various languages reduces efficiency by increasing communication costs and by multiplying expenditures for texts and teaching materials. Those effects are more evident at central educational institutions than at local schools, since central organisms handle larger areas than their local counterparts. On the other hand, the use of various languages can increase administrative instability by raising the uncertainty of results in academic achievement. Since school performance is ultimately viewed as the administrators' responsibility, the uncertainty produced by the increment in educational roles to otherwise relatively minor languages provide incentives for bureaucrats to view with skepticism the inclusion of new languages in education. As with efficiency, the localized expansion of language educational use will increase uncertainty at lower rates than at central, more general levels. This is true because it is easier to collect information from smaller areas and produce policies with more limited and precise scopes.

In sum, administrators' preferences on language policies are influenced by efficiency and stability, and by the levels of decisionmaking. Language diversity increases the potential negative effects on efficiency and stability of educational systems. Hence, educational structures in which decisionmaking lies at the center provide incentives for administrators towards conservatism in educational language use.

Parents

Parents' participation in education may take many forms, such as assisting at home with their children's homework, joining parent-teacher associations, or becoming representatives in school councils. Out of all the actors involved in the educational process, parents are likely to be the least knowledgeable about school operations. This lack of information accounts for a typical reluctance from parents to participate in school decisionmaking processes (Cucchiara and Horvat, 2009; Bauch and Goldring, 1998:21; Fine 1993:697). This reluctance may stem from their belief that they do not have enough knowledge about education and a sense of intimidation from education professionals. Also, parents may not be able to develop a sense of self efficacy (Deslandes and Bertrand, 2005). Socioeconomic status plays a large role in this sense of intimidation, since more educated parents tend to perceive a shorter distance between them and educators than less educated parents (Kohn, 1998; Becker, Nakagawa, and Corwin, 1997). On the other hand, in many instances school administrators and teachers seek parental involvement for crises interventions, in moments where schools' performances are low and parents receive part of the blame for not providing the necessary support at home. Thus, an adversarial relationship between parents and school professionals is not uncommon, based on the dominant model for parental involvement, which ascribes parents an unequal status and a role of supporters and learners of professional educators with little voice in real decisionmaking (Cuchiara and Horvat, 2009; Vincent, 1996:476). More participatory roles for parents are rare, with important exceptions, such as the trendsetting Chicago decentralized school system, placed in effect by legislation in 1989 (Bauch and Goldring, 1998:22; Vincent, 1996; Fine, 1993:700).

Another potential barrier against parental inclusion is the set of demands placed on individuals from other social institutions, such as work and family. For instance, schools may require parents to attend monthly parents-teachers meetings at school, in order to improve overall student achievement. This requirement may force some parents to choose between taking time off from inflexible jobs or losing wages, and attending the school meetings. In other instances, such as those of single parents, becoming involved in their children's school work at home may be unrealistic after working long days with long commutes (Brock and Edmunds, 2010; Fine, 1993:687). Hence, school reforms aimed at increasing parental roles may face challenges that go beyond pedagogical considerations.

Participation from parents may also be hindered by collective action problems presented by the temporary nature of their status as parents of school children. Since children stay in school for a given number of years, the group of parents is constantly changing, so incentives to organize must be continually renewed and even renegotiated.

Parents constitute the most heterogeneous group of all involved in education. Significant differences on parental preferences and effects on children's school performance have been found based on socioeconomic status, educational levels, ethnicity, culture, and gender (Honig, 2004; Bryant, 1998; Kohn, 1998; Lewis, 1995; Casanova, 1996; Dodd, 1996; Vincent, 1996). There are, however, several basic interests that parents share, even if the functional definitions of those interests may vary. For instance, most parents may expect high schools to prepare their children for their future, but differences in work expectations may translate into different school emphases. Individuals in high socioeconomic communities may expect high schools to prepare their children for top ranked universities, while parents from poor neighborhoods may expect the schools to prepare their children to find jobs after graduation or to enter technical schools.

The main interest of parents is the good performance of their own children. Thus, their participation typically begins as a reaction to unsatisfactory performance by their children. This initial individual involvement may turn into a challenge to the politics of public education if systemic characteristics are blamed for the children's unsatisfactory performance (Fine, 1993:699). If parents blame systemic characteristics for their children's problems, the probability increases that they will seek greater roles in school policy decisionmaking. On the other hand, when there is a belief that the poor academic performance of their child is due to a learning problem, the chances of involvement decrease (Deslandes and Bertran, 2005).

Parents also expect schools to help their children reproduce their socioeconomic status or to improve on it (social mobility). Language use on schools is a crucial ingredient in pursuing the interest of social mobility. This interest may take two specific demands on language use. First, parents seek to reproduce their group identity through their children, so they favor the use of their mother tongue, either as language of instruction or as a language course. Second, parents' own experiences with job markets and social mobility opportunities and obstacles, lead them to expect their children to learn the language or languages that will open, or maintain open, the doors to job markets and political participation spaces. This is the case of immigrants who understand that their mother tongue has little social use. In some instances, immigrants may not even want their children to learn their language, believing it would hinder their social mobility opportunities. It is clear, however, that an educational environment in which community interests were included, the belief in the progressive nature of the dominant language would not preclude the use of minority languages. Thus, language preferences include their mother tongue but not at the expense of other languages with social mobility potential. The complexity of a school curriculum allows for the use of more than one language, so parents whose mother tongues have little use in business or government transactions are likely to support the use of more than one language in their children's education.

Since parents do not form a homogeneous group, differences in language use among linguistic groups may present conflicting demands on educational policies. Language minorities may fail to influence educational policy in participatory but centralized systems and in decentralized but non-participatory systems. Participatory but centralized systems tend to favor pressures from majority groups that render smaller groups' efforts ineffective. In decentralized but non-participatory systems, administrators face stronger pressures from state institutions than from parental or community organizations, so the rationalizing logic of state institutions overwhelms minority concerns.

Teachers

There is a strong bias in academic writings in favor of some kind of teachers' inclusion in school management (Mavrogordato, 2012; Hammad and Norris, 2009; Gaziel, 2008; Donato and Tucker, 2007; Conley, 1991). However, specific prescriptions for such participation are varied. There are two main dimensions where teachers may participate: a technical and an administrative dimension (Conley, 1991:226; Mohrman, 1978). The technical dimension refers to specific task executions, such as selecting texts and resolving learning problems (Conley, 1991). The administrative dimension is related to policy decisions and managerial support functions, such as language of instruction, hiring personnel, and assigning budgets. Teachers normally participate in technical domain issues by the nature of their jobs, since they are the only ones who have direct and constant contact with the students,who are the system's clients,. Hence, teachers undertake many procedural decisions on a daily basis, in which it would be logistically inconceivable to constantly consult with their supervisors. However, teachers' rarely have the same participation over administrative and policy decisions.

One of the most striking findings on empirical research about teachers' participation is a tendency towards noninvolvement in policy issues (Hammad and Norris, 2009; Beadie, 1996; Weiss, 1993). Duke, Showers and Imber (1980) have shown how rational calculations may lead only a small number of teachers to become involved in school decisionmaking, even within decentralized systems with shared decisionmaking (SDM) programs, also called "site-based management" (Gaziel, 2008; Castillo and Piñeiro, 2006). Teachers' potential participation costs include increased time demands, loss of autonomy within the classroom, risk of collegial disfavor, subversion of collective bargaining, and threats to career advancement (Duke, et al., 1980:95–97). The advantages, on the other hand, are reduced to feelings of self-efficacy, increased sense of ownership, and exercise of workplace democracy (Duke, et al., 1980:98–99).

The single most important incentive for teachers' participation is the perception of influence on educational policy decisionmaking (Hammad and Norris, 2009; Duke, et al., 1980:104). Given a sense that their involvement will produce an effect on policy outcomes, teachers' benefits of participation increase. Hence, it is more likely that they will participate when their involvement produces tangible results. Influence over policy reduces the probability of collegial disfavor, or that of being seen by peers as being coopted by the administration, it provides a sense that the sacrifices involved with the increased time demands have concrete effects on their jobs and their students' education, and reduces the threats to career advancement by increasing the teachers' share of power within the school system. In a typical strategic decision manner, when the paybacks outweigh the costs, involvement becomes a preference. The neglect of this aspect of human nature has provoked the failure of many decentralization schemes, since they have moved the locus of decisionmaking away from the central office towards the district or school, but have not provided influence for teachers (Castillo and Piñeiro, 2006; Beadie, 1996; Weiss, 1993). Teachers, aware of their lack of effective influence over final outcomes, have sometimes been the strongest opponents of decentralization plans. Beadie (1996) illustrated this point with a school reform project in Illinois in 1992, which faced adamant and adverse reactions from teachers who believed that their influence decreased with the new plan, even if it formally appeared to have expanded their participation in policymaking. Changes in educational structures that provide influence for teachers (at any level) may alter their preferences by reducing the costs of participation, hence creating incentives to become involved.

Teachers' preferences in terms of particular policies may vary, but there is one common element in all of them: job security (Verdugo, et al, 1997; Beadie, 1996). This element stems from the teachers' role as (professional) workers within the service sector. Regardless of policy preferences or pedagogical inclinations, teachers must remain in the job to influence policy, be it technically or administratively. Hence, at any level of decisionmaking, their primary preference will be the maintenance of their jobs. If job security is threatened, everything else is secondary. Work is life. Teachers' unions are particularly important in this respect, since their own existence is often a product of teachers' insecure tenure.

Teachers are also professionals. Their situational and training expertise in classroom matters provide them with a sense of ownership within the classroom that is unmatched by any other group. Teachers' classroom behavior is difficult to supervise on a daily basis, so there is a tendency for teachers to develop a great deal of autonomy. Institutional changes that threaten that autonomy, either by increased supervision or by intervention of non-educators in instructional matters, antagonize the teachers' interests. Thus, while teachers generally favor some kind of influence in policymaking, they oppose it if it is accompanied by losses in classroom autonomy (Beadie, 1996:84; Weiss, 1993).

While noninvolvement may be a tendency for individual teachers, teacher union leaders have strong incentives towards participation in decisionmaking structures. To retain their posts they must become involved in policymaking in the name of the teaching body. However, that involvement may take many forms, from small, local unions to large, central organizations. Leaders of large unions are inclined to favor centralized educational structures where they can have direct influence over policymaking. Since the individual teachers' concern over job security is shared by union leaders, negotiations at central levels provide them with the strength in numbers and wide scale capacity to disrupt the school system's operations, something that would be more difficult with decentralized teachers unions. School decentralization schemes have often been opposed by teachers unions on such grounds. That partly explains why the *Federación de Maestros* and *Asociación de Maestros* opposed the decentralized *Escuelas de la Comunidad*.

Preferences by teachers on language use depend on the language in current use, the potential costs of learning a new language (financial, time, and job security), and of creating new teaching materials if they do not exist. Teachers' participation in low levels of decisionmaking increase the chances of linguistic diversity in education, since teachers are close to and sometimes live in the linguistic communities that send their children to their schools. For those teachers, there are more benefits of adding a language to the school's curriculum than for a centrally based teacher union. The participation of teachers' organizations at centralized levels may tend to follow the state's rationalizing tendency because the costs of using languages other than the central language may outweigh the benefits. Ultimately, then, levels of decisionmaking affect teachers' interests, where low levels reduce the costs of establishing language educational policies that reflect variations in communities' language use, while high levels increase incentives to support language rationalization policies that do not reflect linguistic diversity.

Nonsystem Actors

Coburn (2005) argued that most educational policy studies focused only on system actors and their interactions within the school institutions, from state to school levels. Those studies missed a substantial part of the story since nonsystem actors are also important because they attempt to "promote, translate and transform policy ideas" (Coburn, 2005:23). In fact, nonsystem actors are stronger in educational systems whose institutions allow and encourage the involvement of politics. For instance, San Roman (2013) claims that in the history of public education in Spain, politicians, often with the Catholic Church, have always designed the contents, curriculum, and methodologies of educational policies.

Nonsystem actors include language stakeholders such as nationalist or antinationalist political movements or parties, cultural and human rights organizations, organized civil society groups, intellectuals, and linguistic associations. The nationalist position in colonies tends to confront the imperial language with a native language that becomes dominant. Nationalist preferences in independent states tend to go against the diversity towards minority languages. Organizations and civil society groups that defend linguistic human rights tend to favor diversity over rationalization, while some cultural organizations may provide the ideology that supports the dominant nationalist paradigm, like the Official English movement. Public intellectuals and linguistic associations tend to influence more corpus planning than status or acquisition planning, but the tendency is to reflect their circumstances.

Effects of Educational Institutions on Participation Patterns

Educational systems provide few incentives for non-bureaucratic participation. Teachers' strategic considerations are likely to perceive higher costs than benefits from participation. Involvement in policy decisions increases time commitments for teachers, may place them in adversarial relationships with their supervisors, jeopardize their classroom autonomy, and create resentments from their peers (Weiss, 1993; Duke, et al., 1980). From the parents' perspective, participation in school affairs other than individual support at home may be intimidating based on their perceived lack of knowledge of educational activities compared to that of education professionals. Parental involvement may also be hindered by the potentially conflicting demands from other social institutions, such as jobs and family (Cucchiara and Horvat, 2009; Bauch and Goldring, 1998; Fine, 1993). The administrators' standpoint towards change is influenced by their interest in efficiency, stability, and crisis avoidance (Greenfield, 1995). Changes bring uncertainty and, consequently, increase risks. Thus, bureaucrats tend to approach change cautiously. Bureaucracies are conservative.

At first blush, one would be surprised to find any attempts at non-bureaucratic participation and change in educational policies. It appears that if all actors acted rationally, change in school systems should be a rarity. It is. However, most experts in school matters agree that educational systems should be inclusive and adaptive to new approaches and societal changes (San Román, 2013; Mavrogordato, 2012; Hammad and Norris, 2009; Rey, 2008; Conley, 1991). Educational institutions can help solve this social dilemma, by altering the teachers' and parents' utilities for participating in school politics. Institutions can also reduce the administrators' risks in change and inclusion, thus allowing the groups to derive socially beneficial outcomes from individual rational decisions.

Participation and decentralization are two features of educational systems that may affect a school system's relative capacity to evolve and adapt. Institutional mechanisms that provide non-administrators with influence in educational policies provide incentives for teachers to break the involvement inertia, whether at central offices, through teachers' unions, or at more localized levels through teacher representatives at school councils. Relative centralization does not determine incentives for teachers' participation, but modifies the individual teachers' potential scope of influence in school policies. That is, inclusive decisionmaking structures close to the teachers' communities provide a sense of influence on policies that affect them directly and offer larger prospects for individual teachers to be directly involved in negotiating processes that may be hard to reach in teachers' unions centralized, national-level negotiations. Parents' participation is more unusual and centralized parents' organizations face strong obstacles from collective action problems typical of large groups, like freeriding (Olson, 1971). Smaller-scale participation venues for parents reduce the costs of participation and solve collective action problems, which increases their capacity to organize. Such venues also reduce parents' unequal relationships with school professionals in terms of information about school operations, since they are likely to be better informed about their children's school than about a region or country's whole educational system. Since the unequal informational relationship between parents and educational professionals is a deterrent for parents' involvement, a reduction in the inequality of that relationship may improve the chances of parents' participation. Hence, it appears that parents' relative involvement is directly related to decisionmaking levels, where inclusive institutions closer to local communities are more likely to benefit from parents' incorporation in policymaking than open, but centralized institutions.

Decentralization and Participation Effects on ELAG

Decentralized and participatory educational institutions tend to produce educational policies that reflect a small distance between social and educational uses of language. This is true for three reasons. First, decentralized educational institutions change administrators' incentives and make it more appealing to accept language diversity in education. Second, decentralized structures reduce non-administrators' costs of involvement in policymaking, which increases their drive towards participation and increases the diversity of interests in policymaking. Third, participatory educational structures include non-bureaucratic preferences that may challenge the push towards language rationalization of central administrators. Ultimately the combination of decentralization and participation reduces the administrators' pressures towards pursuing language rationalization policies and permits the influence of local societal sectors that are more sensitive to differences among communities' language use.

Decentralized structures reduce the negative effects on administrative efficiency produced by the use of various languages in education by decreasing the information gathering costs and limiting uncertainty of results. Thus, administrators' preference towards language rationalization losses importance because efficiency and uncertainty are less threatening at local levels than at large-scale central operations.

Decentralized structures reduce non-administrators' costs of involvement in decisionmaking by increasing their influence on policies that affect their communities more directly than those geared towards a wider set of school clients, in which their input would represent a smaller portion of the complete picture. One of the main deterrents for teacher involvement is the risk of taking the chance to participate without exerting concrete influence on educational policies. Decentralized structures reduce that risk and increase the teachers' drive to become involved and even demand reforms to create more open structures.

If decentralization encourages participation, the latter fuels the inclusion of non-bureaucratic preferences that may challenge the drive towards language rationalization of central administrators. Hence, the involvement of groups whose rational calculations drive them to steer away from language rationalization tends to produce educational policies that reflect and respect linguistic diversity. Conversely, structures that don not provide participation incentives for teachers and parents are likely to influence educational language policies with large values of ELAG.

When parents' and teachers' local participation respond to communities' needs, and when administrators face strong demands from non-bureaucrats, educational language policies have a better chance of reflecting the language social use. Thus, the combination of the independent effects of decentralization and participation create favorable conditions for reductions in ELAG.

In sum, there is a theoretical connection between educational structures and language policy outcomes, through the institutional effects on groups' preferences and expected utility payoffs. We can assess the general preferences of the groups involved in educational systems, and evaluate the effects of school systems' institutions on those preferences. A dominant trait of all the three actors involved (administrators, teachers, and parents) is the rational tendency towards conservatism, in terms of participation and change. However, educational institutions that remain exclusive and reluctant to reform are bound to produce suboptimal results. More specifically, inclusion and decentralization can alter the educational groups' conservative tendencies and allow for the establishment of policies that reflect communities' needs without forcing any groups to act against their own rational interests.

The next chapters provide empirical illustrations of the theoretical arguments presented here. They concentrate on the English educational language policy changes in Puerto Rico between 1898 and 2013. The empirical chapters evaluate the effects of participation and decentralization on English language policies during the policy paradigms known as Americanization (1898–1948), Puertoricanization (1949–1968), and Bilingualization (1969–present). They also show how colonial politics impacted the language conflict in Puerto Rico. They present the story behind the theory.

4

The English Question

The history of the use of English in Puerto Rico's educational system provides a fitting example of the relationship between education and politics, and of the political nature of language issues. Since 1898, the use of English in public education has embodied the political relations between the United States and Puerto Rico. Major shifts in educational language policies in Puerto Rico reflected changes in the federal language policy.

Paradigm One: Americanization, 1898–1948

The colonial approach in Puerto Rico was part of a larger wave of Americanization in the U.S. that begun at the end of the 1800s and broke with the tradition of protecting minority language rights (Crawford, 1990). In the mainland, the emphasis was on non-English speaking immigrants, like Germans and Italians, and on Native Americans, like the Cherokee. In the colonies the policy focused on assimilation. In all cases the emphasis was on the coercive teaching of English and it always masked a deeper issue, like racism, religious bigotry, land theft or labor exploitation (Crawford, 1990; Dennis, 1990).

After the U.S. occupation of Puerto Rico, Cuba, the Philippines and the Mariana Islands during the Spanish-Cuban-American War of 1898, the development of a coherent colonial policy became a salient consideration among Washington policymakers. The issue generated public and academic debates that produced a great deal of literature, congressional discussions, executive pronouncements, and even Supreme Court decisions. In the case of Puerto Rico, the objective of Washington's colonial policy was to systematically transform the country's linguistic habits, the administrative structures, the legal system, and the political culture (Cabán, 1998:1).This process became known as the "Americanization" of Puerto Ricans, and the Puerto Rico education department emerged as the main tool of the strategy. The Americanizing intentions of the colonial rulers has been widely documented (Barreto, 2001; Clampitt-Dunlap, 2000; Morales, 2000; Cabán, 1998; López Yustos, 1997; Morris, 1995; Solís, 1994; Negrón de Montilla, 1990; Algren de Gutiérrez, 1987; Cebollero, 1945) and explicitly stated by their enforcers (Clark, 1930; Brumbaugh, 1907). The policy towards the Philippines was also based on an Americanization approach, although the language patterns and results were different (Bauzon, 1991; Benton, 1991; Barrows, 1907). There, English successfully replaced Spanish as the lingua franca of the socioeconomic elite. English in the Philippines, like Spanish before it, could not become more than a secondary language and did not replace the ancient local languages in social use.

The initial focus of the Americanization plan was the introduction of English in schools, in order to replace Spanish as the language of daily use for Puerto Ricans. This approach evolved into maintaining Spanish while establishing English as a primary language. However, while the broad goals were clear, U.S. policymakers did not produce concrete directives, allowing for implementation differences among various colonial administrations. This delegation of authority from U.S. presidents to Puerto Rico's governors and education commissioners created room for variations in educational language policies. The result was three major educational language policies during the Americanization period until it was abandoned shortly after World War II.

The Early Years: The Eaton/Clark Policy, 1898–1904

John Eaton (1898–1899) was the first man in charge of education during the American military occupation. Together with Victor Clark (1899–1900), initially his assistant and later his replacement, Eaton established the tone for the next fifty years of language policies. The tone was one of molding what they believed was an ignorant population into a democratic and productive people with strong American values. Learning English was an essential aspect of the Americanizing goals, and the department played a unique role in its implementation. Eaton had close ties with the Carlisle Indian Industrial School in Pennsylvania, which pursued the Americanization of Native Americans (Navarro-Rivera, 2006). The public schools would do to Puerto Ricans what Carlisle did to Native Americans.

The first educational institution created by the military regime was the education bureau, under the U.S. department of the interior. The military governor of Puerto Rico, Major General Guy V. Henry, following Eaton's recommendations, promulgated the first School Laws in May 1, 1899, based on the educational laws of Massachusetts (Dexter, 1908). They established a transitional organization from the Spanish to the American system, in which school districts were encouraged, although not required, to create new schools. School boards retained the authority to hire teachers, and the responsibility to provide their pay and housing. School boards were also responsible for the selection, rent, and equipment of school buildings (Solís, 1994:58; Osuna, 1949).

Commissioners Eaton and Clark introduced English as a language course from first grade and established it as the language of instruction for middle and high school. Since middle and high schools were non existent for most people outside San Juan, they were mostly affected by the introduction of language courses. The Foraker Act approved by the U.S. congress in 1900 created a civil government for Puerto Rico and institutionalized the centralized nature of the department that has lasted until our days. Through subsequent school laws, school boards lost their autonomy and faded away quickly.

The first commissioner of education under the civil government was Martin Brumbaugh (1900–1901), who enacted a new educational language policy in 1900. Instruction would be in Spanish from first to eighth grade, and English, from eighth through twelfth grade. Brumbaugh also arranged for Puerto Rican students to attend Carlisle, Hampton, Tuskegee, and other institutions that educated Indians and Colored people in the U.S. (Rosa, 2003; Navarro-Rivera, 2006). Commissioner Samuel Lindsay (1902–1904) maintained Brumbaugh's policy.

English at Any Price: The Falkner Policy, 1904–1916

Roland Falkner (1904–1907) established a new language policy in the academic year of 1905–1906. The emphasis on English instruction grew in new and larger proportions. He decreed English as the medium of instruction in all classes starting on second grade. Rural schools, poorer than their urban counterparts and lacking enough teachers trained in English, experienced the transition at a slower pace. His tenure lasted only until 1907, but his policy extended until 1916 with the next three commissioners, Edwin Dexter, Edward Bainter, and Paul Miller. The English impulse came at the expense of Spanish, which was reduced to one daily class period. The approval of a new school law in 1905, product of Falkner's efforts, made it mandatory for Puerto Rican teachers to pass an annual English exam to receive their teaching licenses.

Initially, the policy only faced moderate adverse reactions because of a unique political juncture produced by an alliance between the colonial governor and the leading political sectors in Puerto Rico. Before Falkner, Commissioners Brumbaugh and Lindsay had provoked hostile public reactions from Puerto Rican politicians and educators by their crude emphases on English instruction and Americanization tactics. Also, the limited Foraker Act of 1900 that created a civil government for Puerto Rico alleviated briefly the claims for self-government that most Puerto Ricans believed would accompany the United States' sovereignty. Particularly salient in the public debate was the possibility of U.S. citizenship for Puerto Ricans. In an effort to manage the island's negative public opinion, President Theodore Roosevelt named Beeckman Winthrop governor of Puerto Rico (1904–1907), with the intention to improve political relations with the Puerto Rican leading politicians. Winthrop cultivated good terms with the leaders of the newly formed *Partido Unión,* which incorporated most politicians in favor of some form of self-government and recognition of the Puerto Rican culture (Negrón de Montilla, 1990; Bayrón Toro, 1984). The *Partido Unión* held control of the legislature from 1904 to 1928, and Winthrop placed several of its leaders in high government posts. Consequently, while generally opposing Americanizing strategies, the *Unionistas* moderated their criticisms against the language policy. The opposition party, the pro-statehood *Partido Republicano*, lost its privileged position within the island's government apparatus and gave way to the *Partido Unión* as the majority party. *Republicano* leaders protested the party's loss of influence within Governor Winthrop's cabinet to *Unionistas*. However, the party's position as defender of the island's inclusion in the U.S. federation prevented them from rejecting the Americanizing tactics, which they considered necessary to facilitate the island's annexation. The platform of the *Partido Republicano* from 1899 argued that English should be taught in schools because it "will soon be the official language" of the island, and that it would place Puerto Rico "in more favorable conditions, soon to become a new state" of the union (in Morris, 1995:24). Hence, during Falkner's tenure, his language policy did not face the kind of hostility that other commissioners encountered after him. The largest adverse reaction to the policy would come after Falkner himself was out of office.

Commissioner Dexter (1907–1912) continued and intensified Falkner's policy, stressing English instruction in rural schools, extending the use of English as the medium of instruction to first grade, and eliminating Spanish courses from the first grade curriculum. His efforts towards rural school instruction and emphasis on courses in agricultural skills and hygiene were significant since the majority of the island's population lived away from the coastal urban centers of San Juan, Ponce, Mayagüez, and Arecibo. Dexter's tenure coincided with the peak of the *Partido Unión's* power after a landslide victory in the 1908 legislative elections. By then the new governor Regis Post had effectively terminated the alliance with the *Unionistas*, who became disappointed by their unfulfilled expectations of increased self-government during Winthrop's administration. The opposition grew. The *Asociación de Maestros de Puerto Rico* (AMPR) was created in 1912 as the first national teachers' union. The AMPR immediately took among its main campaigns the elimination of English as the medium of instruction in schools, and forged an alliance with leaders of the *Partido Unión*, who took their claims to the legislature. The AMPR's posture did not preclude that many teachers would take advantage of the incentives provided by the department to become trained in English instruction, such as higher salaries and better career opportunities. For instance, during the academic year 1909–1910, 124 rural teachers, most of them Puerto Rican, asked for and obtained permission from their supervisors to offer all their schools' courses in English (Negrón de Montilla, 1990). However, the AMPR represented the widespread concern about the individual costs on teachers in terms of time and resources in order to learn English and adapt to the new imported teaching methods,[1] and about the anti-pedagogical nature of the English language policy.

The resistance reached its zenith during Bainter's tenure (1912–1915). By then the English language policy had become a major public debate, known as *el problema del idioma* or the English problem. Bainter continued the language policy virtually unchanged; only establishing Spanish as the medium of instruction for elementary school courses in Nature Study, and Health and Hygiene. The AMPR's links with the *Partido Unión* were confirmed after the former's general assembly in December 1912, which agreed to petition from the Puerto Rico house of delegates legislation in favor of the use of Spanish in schools. Resulting partly from the AMPR's efforts, the house approved in 1913 a bill establishing Spanish as the language of instruction in elementary schools (which extended to eighth grade), and a bill eliminating the annual English requirement for teaching licenses. The strongest opposition to the bills came from Representative Juan B. Huyke, who later became commissioner of education. The conflict was complicated by a bill presented in the U.S. congress considering the extension of U.S. citizenship to Puerto Ricans, which provoked a new wave of public discussions regarding the issue of Puerto Rican national identity within the political relations with the United States . The executive council (upper house) vetoed the house of delegates' language bills, effectively maintaining Falkner's policy. The house approved another language bill in 1915, which strived to make Spanish the language of instruction and of the courts, only to be vetoed again by the executive council. Although no other language bill would pass in either legislative chamber until 1946, the language debate remained intrinsically linked to the larger questions of national identification and colonialism.

It's Not That Easy: The Miller/Huyke Policy, 1916–1934

Woodrow Wilson named Paul Miller commissioner of education (1915–1921). The AMPR, the *Unionistas*, and the *Republicanos* welcomed him because it ended Bainter's polemic tenure and offered new hope for a different tone. His appointment sparked a series of favorable articles in the Puerto Rican press from both conservative (The Porto Rico Progress) and liberal (*La Democracia*) sides; a significant departure form the hostile press treatment received by his predecessor. Miller's first message to Puerto Rico's teachers, published in *La Democracia*, official periodical of the *Unionistas*, expressed much respect towards the profession. He also showed a great deal of respect towards Puerto Rican culture, as evidenced in a letter addressed to the American teachers in the island:

> Since many of you are new to the work this year, I desire to make a few suggestions for your guidance, not only in the school room, but in your relations with the people of the community where you are teaching... Cultivate the acquaintance of the best people of your community and mingle among them... You are particularly requested to refrain from criticizing local habits, customs and conditions that are new and strange to you, especially in your home papers. Such articles are sure to be forwarded to our local press by clipping bureaus to your own chagrin. Remember that the people of Porto Rico are no worse than we are, but they are different (Circular Letter 11, 1915).

In 1916 Miller established a new language policy, in which Spanish would be the medium of instruction for most classes until fourth grade. Fifth grade would include classes in Spanish and English, while grades sixth and higher would have English as the medium of instruction, except for Physiology and Spanish. The policy reversed some aspects, but stopped short of the AMPR's and *Partido Unión's* goals of using

Spanish as the instructional medium until at least high school. An important theoretical justification was the publication of José Padín's 1916 study of the educational system that criticized Falkner's policy and proposed the use of Spanish as instructional medium in all grades with English as a special subject (López Yustos, 1997:139). Padín, a prominent school supervisor who later became education commissioner, was the first scholar to produce a systematic research of the island's educational conditions.

Miller's honeymoon with the teachers' union came to an end after his new policy failed to meet the high expectations from the AMPR. The AMPR criticized him in their 1917 annual assembly and approved a resolution demanding the use of Spanish as instructional medium in all grades (Negrón de Montilla, 1990:173), which provoked a public response from Miller justifying his changes. While the tone of the public discussion was deferential, the main differences were clear.

Another source of friction was a rise of Puerto Rican nationalism spurred by the disappointment of many societal sectors with the limitations of the Jones Act of 1917. The Jones Act replaced the Foraker Act of 1900, creating an elected senate and separating the governor's cabinet from the legislative process. However, it did not allow the Puerto Rican electorate to choose its governor. Since the school system had been linked to the relations with the U.S. since 1898, the rising nationalism penetrated the individual schools. Student and teacher activism took the form of defense of Puerto Rican symbols. Students demanded the raising of the single-star Puerto Rican flag in several high school graduation ceremonies. The single-star flag had been used by the pro-independence movement during the latter stages of the Spanish sovereignty, and was not welcomed by American authorities. The insistence from students in some high schools on using the Puerto Rican symbols, and the search for signatures supporting legislative measures in favor of Spanish as the instructional medium, motivated Miller to suspend several students. Reactions against the suspensions included student strikes, teacher activism, and the creation by José De Diego of a private high school that used Spanish as the instructional medium (Morris, 1995; Negrón de Montilla, 1990). Miller suppressed the student strikes and made public that no teacher supporting the independence movement would be hired by the department. In fact, he compiled a list of graduating students from the Normal School of Puerto Rico, which trained school teachers, who participated in public demonstrations supporting independence. No teacher from that list would be hired. The requirement of open loyalty to the U.S. to be a teacher in Puerto Rico's public school system controlled much of the teaching activism, but provided an important tool for popular sympathy towards the AMPR's postures.

Miller was replaced by Huyke (1921-1930), a prominent *Unionista* and former member of the Puerto Rico house of representatives who supported the Americanization plan. He was the first Puerto Rican to become commissioner of education. While the volume and tone of Commissioner Huyke's expressions about the need to learn English appeared almost obsessive, the curriculum was not changed substantially, except from an increase in the allotted time for English classes in rural schools. However, he emphasized the use of English in other areas. An oral English exam became mandatory for high school graduation and all official departmental communication had to be written in English. He continued the practice of not hiring teachers openly identified with the independence movement.

A 1925 study by the Teachers' College of Columbia University, commissioned by the Puerto Rican legislature, concluded that the policy was unjustified and recommended that no English courses should be taught until fourth grade, and that English as the medium of instruction should not start before seventh grade. The findings also stressed the favorable public opinion in Puerto Rico towards learning English, a fact generally ignored by the movement against teaching English in schools (Algren de Gutiérrez, 1987:84). It became part of the public debate and furnished the policy opponents with a solid tool to strengthen their arguments. However, Huyke rejected the findings and continued with his language policy. Relations with the AMPR deteriorated and reached their lowest point at the annual convention in 1926. The AMPR demanded a new classification and hiring system that would reduce the commissioner's arbitrary decisions. It also demanded the elimination of the English policy and rejected the use of Huyke's own books in the classroom. He responded by advising the department's teaching personnel to abstain from participating in the AMPR's activities, a stark departure from Miller's position:

> The last General Convention of the Teachers' Association of Porto Rico assumed an unfriendly and disrespectful attitude toward the Department of Education and the school organization in general. Under the circumstances, this office is obliged to advise you not to take any further active participation in the affairs of the Teachers' Association (Circular Letter 75, 1927).

The strong rhetoric in favor of American values antagonized members of his party, the AMPR, and the nationalist sector (Negrón de

Montilla, 1990). He made no apologies for his views and believed in a permanent union with the U.S., and professed loyalty to what he considered its progressive and democratic history. He also opposed several bills that tried to decentralize the department and reduce the commissioner's power (Negrón de Montilla, 1990:241). His postures received the support of the *Republicanos* and the *Partido Socialista Obrero*[2]. The Miller/Huyke educational language policy remained in place for 18 years.

The Decline of Americanization: The Padín Policy, 1934–1948

Padín was designated commissioner of education by President Hoover in 1930. He had occupied several supervisory positions under Miller's and Huyke's administrations. In fact, his Master's thesis, published in 1915, influenced the public debate over the educational use of English. Miller himself had it to justify the policy change of 1916.

The climate surrounding the naming of Padín resembled that of Miller's appointment in 1915. Like Miller, he replaced a conflictive administrator who, regardless of his policies' merits, had not managed to establish either a favorable public opinion or an effective power base within the educational system. Also like Miller, he rose through the department's ranks and was perceived by most as an insider who knew the school system from personal experience. Both men sparked favorable reactions after their appointments, and both raised expectations about potential educational reforms. The AMPR's president, Gerardo Sellés, praised him and expressed positive expectations about his tenure. The new commissioner's biography appeared on several newspapers and his views on education received much editorial attention (López Yustos, 1997:150; Negrón de Montilla, 1990:247). He announced a new educational language policy that made Spanish the language of instruction for all grades in elementary school, which extended until eighth grade. Padín explained:

> All subjects in the elementary school, with the exception of English, shall be taught in Spanish. English will be offered from the first grade up. The time given to English has been increased 100% in the upper grades so that intensive instruction in that subject may be given. We are confident that this change will result in better instruction in both the subjects that are to be taught in Spanish and in English itself (Circular Letter 10, 1934).

Public reactions to the new policy varied. Language stakeholders who had traditionally opposed emphases on English applauded it and called him "the first true Puerto Rican Commissioner of Education," in obvious reference to Huyke, whom they did not consider a "true Puerto Rican" because of his stress on English use and U.S. values (Algren de Gutiérrez, 1987; Cebollero, 1945). Supporters included the AMPR, the newly created Students Federation (which requested that it be extended to high schools as well) and the *Unionistas*. Among his foes were those who favored stronger ties with the United States, particularly *Republicanos* and *Socialistas*. However, not only pro-American groups opposed the language policy. The pro-independence *Nacionalistas* also criticized it, since they believed it accommodated too much to American demands. For the *Nacionalistas*, even the inclusion of English courses was unacceptable since it only contributed to American imperialism (Algren de Gutiérrez, 1987:96).

Commissioner José M. Gallardo (1937–1945) was a professor of Modern Languages in South Carolina who had worked as a rural teacher and school supervisor in the Puerto Rican public school system. He received instructions from President Franklin Roosevelt to stress the teaching of English. Roosevelt addressed a letter to Gallardo expressing the desire to develop a bilingual population in Puerto Rico (López Yustos, 1997:162; Osuna, 1949; Cebollero, 1945:27). While the statements did not specify any clear policy changes, they represented the first time that a president had written formally to an education commissioner on the language subject. Gallardo interpreted it as a rejection of Padín's policy and a demand for a reversal of his use of Spanish as instructional medium. As a result, he began in 1937 a brief period of pedagogical experiments. From 1937 to 1940 Spanish was used as instructional medium for all courses in the first two grades, for two thirds of the courses in the third and fourth grades, in half the courses in the fifth and sixth grades, and in one third of the courses in the seventh and eighth grades. The remainder courses were taught in English, and all high school was taught in English. From 1940 to 1942 Spanish was the instructional medium in the first two grades and English was the instructional medium in grades seven and eight. In grades three through six, there was one session, with all courses in Spanish, and a second session, with English as a "related subject," where the subjects in the first session were reviewed in English (Osuna, 1949:380).

The changes never amounted to a coherent educational language policy, and reflected a desire to address Washington's concerns and the language stakeholders' demands rather than a conviction in a specific plan. In the school year of 1942–1943, Gallardo returned to the policy of using Spanish as the instructional medium in all grades of the elementary school, effectively returning to Padín's policy (Osuna, 1949). His experiments modified the approach for several years, but did not become a clear and distinct language policy. Their complexity created uncertainty and even confusion among supervisors and teachers, who were ultimately responsible for their enforcement. Hence, the changes were never fully implemented. It must be noted that most scholars on Puerto Rican education do not include Gallardo's years as part of Padín's policy (López Yustos, 1997; Morris, 1995; Algren de Gutiérrez, 1987; Rodríguez Bou, 1960; Osuna, 1949; Cebollero, 1945), so the interpretation presented here represents an alternative explanation to the traditional classification of educational language policies in Puerto Rico. While they all consider Gallardo's years a policy on their own, they also acknowledge the uncertain and confusing nature of his reforms and the difficulties provoked by their enforcement. Thus, based on the inconsistency, short life, and reversal of the approach, his whole tenure is included here within the policy period that lasted until 1948, when Villaronga established a new educational language policy.

Paradigm Two: Puertoricanization, 1949–1968

The Puertoricanization paradigm became possible after the abandonment of the Americanization policy in the U.S. during the 1940s. The perceived threat in the U.S. public opinion of non assimilated immigrants had waned and the federal government had relaxed its practice of coercive English education. The colonial policy reflected the shift and the island's political administrators acquired more leverage over Puerto Rico's educational language policies (Crawford, 1990).

Puerto Ricans elected their governor for the first time in 1948 by virtue of the Law of Elected Governor approved by the U.S. Congress in 1947. The law provided that the governor would name its full cabinet, particularly the commissioner of education and the attorney general, which had been appointed by the president since 1900. The emergent ruling coalition, led by Governor Luis Muñoz Marín and the *Partido Popular Democrático* (PPD), established a populist government based on a particular notion of Puerto Rican cultural nationalism. The PPD administration adopted several symbols related to the independence movement, such as the flag, the anthem, and the language. Spanish was confirmed as part of the attempt at constructing the new Puerto Rican identity. Muñoz Marín's own wife, Inés Mendoza, had been a public school teacher and supporter of Spanish as a medium of instruction. The new Puerto Rican identity imagined a common past based on the life of the white, poor, small peasant of the interior, the *jíbaro*. His silhouette adorned the PPD's flag. The new imaginary removed from the political past the claims for independence by the political nationalists in Puerto Rico's history. The Puerto Rican Independence Party, a breakup of the PPD, and the Nationalist Party, a movement that led an attack on the U.S. Congress itself in 1954, rejected the PPD's avoidance of what they believed was the natural conclusion of the affirmation of a distinct Puerto Rican nationality: sovereignty. The challenge of the independence parties was the biggest political threat to the PPD's political control. The *Partido Independentista Puertorriqueño* was the second largest party in 1952 and represented a potential loss of votes from the large pro-independence sector of the PPD. Hence, Muñoz Marín and his associates had to walk a fine line between the political and the cultural nationalism, maintaining in the same party the pro and anti independence ideologies.

Nevertheless, Puerto Rico experienced changes in the way the government was administered. The government bureaucracy was transformed from one dominated by English speakers to one dominated by Spanish speakers, particularly at supervisory levels. The education department experienced the replacement of American by Puerto Rican bureaucrats from prominent posts.

The U.S. territorial policy during this period was influenced by the cold war and the emergence of the United Nations. The U.S. ambassador to the United Nations, Henry Cabot Lodge, Jr. managed to have the General Assembly approve Resolution 748 in 1953 declaring that Puerto Rico had obtained self-rule and that the United States could cease to submit reports to the UN about it. This act deflated the international pressure to resolve the colonial problem with the island and gave the autonomists a great boost.

Puertoricanization meant the replacement of a significant sector of the government bureaucracy who were Americans and were largely monolingual English speakers. Many Americans lost their jobs while many more Puerto Ricans earned one. The department reduced the budget for English programs and reduced the influence of the English supervisors in matters of policy.

Muñoz Marín's government, like all other Latin American populist regimes, depended on the strength of the ruling corporatist coalition. The coalition included a centralized labor sector that organized in government sponsored unions. Like Cárdenas in Mexico, Muñoz Marín included the rural sector in his coalition. Unlike Perón in Argentina, Muñoz Marín did not have the overwhelming support of the middle urban class. The ruling coalition also included several public corporations and private entrepreneurs. The AMPR became one of the unions associated with the PPD, which meant an increase in the union's influence and participation in the department's decisionmaking processes, particularly the language issue.

The ruling coalition, however, excluded several important workers unions, prominent entrepreneurs and bankers, like Luis A. Ferré and Miguel García Méndez, urban professionals, the middle class, and the urban poor. These groups represented a minority until the late 1960s, when the populist coalition dissolved and they took power with the *Partido Nuevo Progresista* (PNP). The pro-statehood PNP then replaced the Puertoricanization paradigm with one of Bilingualization.

The department of education experienced an important change when the power to nominate and confirm the education commissioner moved from Washington to San Juan in 1949. The new commissioner of education, Villaronga (1946–1947; 1949–1957) fulfilled the nationalists' claim that Spanish become the sole medium of instruction in the public school system. In 1950 the U.S. congress authorized the government of Puerto Rico to create its own constitution. The new constitution was ratified by a popular vote in 1952. It changed the name from Education Department to Department of Public Instruction, but did not change the institution itself. It remained a highly centralized department.

Reversal of Fortunes: The Villaronga Policy, 1949–1968

In 1946 Puerto Rico's legislature went over the governor's veto to approve a bill establishing Spanish as the medium of instruction. President Truman, however, upheld the veto and nullified the bill. That same year he nominated Villaronga for commissioner of education. The U.S. senate delayed the confirmation in response to his pro-Spanish views expressed during the congressional hearings to review his nomination. He resigned but returned in 1949, this time nominated by the governor of Puerto Rico and confirmed by its senate (López Yustos, 1997:174).

Villaronga enjoyed the enthusiastic support of the language stakeholders that supported Spanish, most of whom belonged to the ruling populist coalition. His policy reduced the educational use of English and increased that of Spanish. He made large curriculum changes and replaced most textbooks, particularly those of Social Studies, History and Spanish courses. The Villaronga educational language policy established Spanish as the medium of instruction for all grades in grammar school, middle school, and high school. It maintained English as a "special subject" with a daily language course for all grades and no presence as a medium of instruction. There were no specialized bilingual schools either at the time.

Villaronga's policy established several reforms related to the role of English in the public school system (López Yustos, 1997:175,190). First, English ceased to be used as a medium of instruction. Second, the department of education stopped recruiting English teachers from the U.S. Third, he instituted the *departmentalization* of English teaching at the elementary level. This meant that only specialized teachers could teach English. Soon this practice became extensive to other areas like Math, Science, and Spanish. Fourth, the policy eliminated the post of English supervisor and the privileges it entailed. Fifth, the department created afternoon English conversational courses for adults who planned to migrate to the U.S. in order to support the government's policy of encouraging emigration as a tool to reduce the unemployment in Puerto Rico. Through the extent of Villaronga's language policy the methodology to teach English was that of a tertiary and sometimes foreign language, a big departure from the Americanization era.

The *Academia Puertorriqueña de la Lengua* was founded in 1955 with Villaronga's support. The new academy avoided the link between the political status and the language controversy. This is another example of the cultural nationalism overtaking the political nationalism. It stands in contrast with the *Academia Antillana de la Lengua,* which José De Diego, a pro-independence leader, had proposed in 1915. It focused on the cultural and political traits that made us similar to Cuba and the Dominican Republic, but different from the United States.

Villaronga showed great vision with the creation of a government television channel, WIPR/WIPM, inaugurated a year after he left office. It was the first station in Latin America that was dedicated to educational programming. The channel belonged to the department and presented instructive shows that may not have been aired on commercial channels. It even aired shows that prepared people for high school equivalency tests. The person who materialized his vision was Efraín Sánchez Hidalgo (1957–1959). A social psychologist with a Ph.D. from Columbia University, Sánchez Hidalgo enjoyed much prestige within the academic community. However, his tenure was shorter than his predecessor and established no considerable changes in the educational language policy. He renewed the emphasis on the program for adult education, which included English conversational courses for potential migrants. He also encouraged the involvement of parents as supporters of the learning process.

Sánchez Hidalgo was replaced by Cándido Oliveras in 1960. Secretary Oliveras (1960–1964) was not a teacher, so he relied heavily on his under secretary, Angel Quintero, who replaced him in 1965. Oliveras continued with Villaronga's policy, emphasized the afternoon English courses, and introduced English classes on television via WIPR. He instituted other secondary measures regarding English, such as replacing the reading textbooks by those responding to a newer methodology, providing scholarships for teachers to study English in the U.S., and creating the Institute for English as a Second Language at the University of Puerto Rico for grammar school English teachers. Oliveras attempted to extend the language policy to private schools, many of which used English as a medium of instruction. A public controversy emerged which involved a group denominated by the Society Bishop Arizmendi, which supported the use of Spanish in private education; U.S. Representative Clayton Powell, who threatened with withdrawing the federal funds assigned to P.R.'s public education; Oliveras, who supported the use of Spanish in private schools; and Muñoz Marín, who rejected Oliveras' public expressions. In the end nothing was done and the private schools were allowed to continue teaching in any language they so preferred, as long as they included Spanish and English language courses.

Quintero's administration (1965–68) coincided with the decline of the populist era. His tenure was characterized by the attempts at pedagogical innovations, such as individualized teaching, schools without grades, and model schools. Besides establishing teacher exchange programs with some U.S. states, the English policy remained unchanged. He created a variety of advanced English courses for high school seniors, such as American Literature, Drama, and a Modified Basic Course in English, Composition, and Oral Communication.

Paradigm Three: Bilingualization, 1969–Present

Most work on the English question in Puerto Rico presumes that the Villaronga policy still rules. For instance, López-Laguerre (1997:40) stated unequivocally that "Villaronga's policy is the one that has prevailed until our day." However, I propose that in 1969 a new paradigm emerged that changed the nature of the English language policies in the department. The new paradigm was that of Bilingualization, in which the political language stakeholders supporting English emerged with new strength, aided by several historical developments. The Bilingual Education Act of 1968, a byproduct of President Lyndon Johnson's Great Society, created Title VII and promoted bilingual schools around the nation (Schmidt, 2000:13). In 1974 the Supreme Court declared in Lau vs. Nichols that in order for students to receive the same quality of public education their instruction should be in their mother language (Schmidt, 2000). The Title VII program and the "Lau remedies" funded and legitimized bilingual schools in Puerto Rico. The new federal approach to language in education merged with the return migration of thousands of Puerto Rican children and adults from the U.S. who spoke little or no English, which in turn increased the demand for bilingual programs. This also helped in the *federalization* of the department through the rapidly increasing dependence on U.S. grants. Eventually the federal view of education would limit the options over educational policies in Puerto Rico. Another historical development was the end of the perception of threat by the English language. English was no longer a menace for Puerto Rican culture as it had been in the past, product of two decades of using Spanish as the medium of instruction. Finally, the end of the populist coalition and the emergence of a strong pro-statehood movement brought to power political elites that rejected the cultural nationalism project and its emphasis on Spanish as a symbol of Puerto Rican identity. Nevertheless, the PPD kept using the defense of Spanish over English as a way to appeal to the pro-independence sectors and to block statehood advances.

The 1968 elections broke the populist era with the victory of a pro-statehood party, the newly created PNP. For the first time the Puerto Rican language stakeholders that favored Americanization and the use of English as a medium of instruction were in a position to name the secretary of instruction and determine educational policy. The new governor, Luis A. Ferré (1969–1972), named Ramón Mellado Parsons (1969–1972). Mellado dedicated attention to English education, increased the program's funds, and hired English teachers and assistants from the U.S., paid with federal grants.

The elections of 1968 saw the epiphany of a bipartisan system in which two parties shared 95 percent of the vote. Contrary to the period between 1948 and 1968, no party has been able to dominate the electoral process indefinitely. However, when it comes to language politics the pro-independence and autonomist sectors have unified against the pro-statehood to reject the use of English as a medium of instruction. On the other hand, the attempts to reduce the educational role of English have also provoked the coalition of the pro-statehood movement and a fraction of the autonomist sector to reject the elimination of English as a language course.

The period between 1985 and 1991 experienced a surge of cultural nationalism aided by an attempt to establish a language policy that placed Spanish above English in official and real status. However, the language stakeholders against the establishment of Spanish-only policies at the expense of English prevented it from being fully developed and implemented.

The cultural nationalist revival was confronted by a surge in pro-Americanism during the *Rossellato*, as has been termed Rosselló's tenure between 1993 and 2000. There was a push towards statehood that spilled over to the language policies. His first piece of legislation returned English to an equal legal status with Spanish. The educational policy attempted to reestablish English's role as a medium of instruction in the public school system of Puerto Rico.

The English Problem Resurfaces: The Mellado Policy, 1969–1996

Mellado's 1969 policy increased the educational role of English by creating bilingual schools, which reintroduced the use of English as a medium of instruction, albeit in a much smaller scale than before. He established a transitional bilingual program, designed to help Anglophone returning migrants from the U.S. to become integrated in a system with Spanish as a medium of instruction. A letter addressed to regional directors, superintendents and school principals indicated:

> The number of Puerto Rican students that return from the United States to join our educational system has increased considerably during recent years. These pupils in many cases speak English as their first language. In other cases, they speak Spanish with some fluidity, but with great limitations in reading and writing (Circular Letter 127, 1969).

The public reaction to the new policy resembled that of the Americanization years. Those in favor linked the use of English to the safeguard of the American citizenship and the ideals it represented. Also, the excitement that blanketed the pro-statehood movement after its historic electoral feat gave it hope to achieve their ultimate objective. It was clear to them that the relatively small social and educational uses of English in Puerto Rico would give their opponents in the U.S. congress and the executive a strong weapon against statehood. However, in spite of all the rhetoric, the educational language policy fell short of provoking cultural assimilation.

It seems clear from Mellado's pronouncements and writings that he favored a much larger role for English in the school system than he actually implemented. That is, he would have favored the reintroduction of English as the medium of instruction on a large scale. The Puerto

Rican society however, did not share his view, although it showed a greater affinity towards the concept of bilingualism. This new consensus, regardless of political preference, characterizes the post-Puertoricanization period of educational language policies.

The issue of English instruction assumed a secondary role through the administrations of Celeste Benítez (1973) and Ramón Cruz (1973–1976). In fact, between 1973 and 1976 the topic virtually disappeared from the circular letters.

The next few secretaries of instruction seemed more preoccupied with obtaining federal grants for educational programs than with altering the educational language policy. In fact, Secretary Carlos Chardón (1977–1979) was partly named for his skills as a grant seeker and his connections in Washington, in spite of having no experience as a teacher (López Yustos, 1997:329). By the end of the 1970s the federal grants accounted for almost half the budget of the department of education.

The Bilingualization was tested during the second administration of Governor Rafael Hernández Colón (1985–1992), who felt forced to rely on Spanish as a symbol of cultural nationalism against the pressure from the U.S. congress to consider statehood for Puerto Rico. Barreto (2001) claims that Hernández Colón's emphasis on Spanish against English appears to be irrational from an electoral perspective, given that public opinion was against it. However it is very rational if he used it to provoke the *English Only* movement to reject the statehood for Puerto Rico during the congressional hearings that were being held in Washington. In fact, it did just that. During his tenure as governor the language policy followed a nationalist path: Secretary Aponte Roque's reduction in English use, the elimination of English as an official language, and the celebration of a failed referendum to amend the constitution of Puerto Rico in order to include the protection of the Puerto Rican culture and the Spanish language. The intensity of the public debate that emerged during his tenure had not been seen since the times of the Americanization policy.

Under this context Aponte Roque (1985–1988) announced in 1985 that she would intensify the use of Spanish and that some schools would experiment with eliminating the English language courses from the first three grades. The *Asociación de Maestros* and the *Federación de Maestros* supported the change. The *Asociación de Escuelas Privadas de Puerto Rico,* which included most of the private bilingual schools and to whom the policy did not affect directly, opposed it (Barreto, 2001:55). The policy never took effect due to the effective opposition from a coalition of nonsystem language stakeholders that overwhelmed Aponte Roque's intentions.

Hernández Colón did not run for a third consecutive term and his party lost the next election, due in large part to his unpopular rejection of the English language and the polarization provoked by his nationalism. The return of the pro-statehood party to the governorship, with a decisive victory of Pedro Rosselló over Victoria Muñoz, the daughter of Muñoz Marín, gave much impetus to the assimilationist movement. Governor Rosselló (1993–2000) acted as a language stakeholder since his first law, which increased the social use of English. He also promoted statehood by holding a plebiscite on the political status only a few months after taking the oath. However, he surprised most people by naming as secretary of education a known politician, member of the opposition party PPD.

José Arsenio Torres (1993–1994) was a Political Science college professor who had also been an active politician and member of the Puerto Rico senate, always opposing statehood. He had also sided with the language stakeholders who supported the use of Spanish as a medium of instruction. Nevertheless, there was an agreement on the need to reform the institutions of the school system, and the idea of the *Escuelas de la Comunidad* was born with Law 18 of 1993. There are many circular letters under Secretary Torres' signature that deal with decentralization and participation. However, those relating to the English question are virtually absent, which indicates that either the issue was secondary to Torres or it was a potential source of conflict with the governor. In fact, Torres remained in his post only until 1994, and was replaced by a man with no ideological conflicts with Rosselló or the ruling party.

A Bilingual Citizen: The Fajardo Policy, 1996–2000

Rosselló established a new language policy that included: a new educational policy with English immersion programs; the reinstatement of English as an official language; and the use of English in many official affairs.

Rosselló took no chances with the next secretary and named Victor Fajardo (1994-2000), an active member of the PNP who was willing to enforce the new language policy and promote statehood from the school system. The Fajardo policy represented an attempt to capitalize in the growing public perception that knowledge of English was an important skill for social mobility opportunities in Puerto Rico. There was a general assumption among many societal sectors that it was more relevant for a person's chances in the job market than the knowledge of High Spanish. The policy reduced the incentives to learn High Spanish and increased those to learn High English. The tragedy lied in that many children failed to learn English at a reasonable rate and did not receive the emphasis on their native language, Spanish to compete effectively in that sector of the job market where knowledge of High Spanish is vital.

The Fajardo policy proposed the creation of a bilingual citizen by establishing partial immersion schools, which he termed bilingual. The *Proyecto Para Formar un Ciudadano Bilingüe (*1997), was a researched but propagandistic theoretical justification of the policy. It announced the introduction of English as a medium of instruction for Science and Mathematics classes. It also approached the methodology of teaching English as that of a primary language. The policy ignited another public, political and intellectual debate around *the English question.* In contrast with the Mellado Policy of 1969, the new bilingual program did not focus on transition but on immersion. It was not designed to integrate English speakers to an all-Spanish education, but rather to immerse Spanish speakers into an English medium. It stated that:

> In spite of the efforts taken by the Department of Education, the truth is that the language is not being learned in our schools, with the emphasis it requires. Even when the students take English courses for 50 minutes a day during their twelve years in school, at the end of their senior year in high school, 90% of them cannot sustain a simple conversation in English. Among other reasons, this is because English is not in its natural environment, and one is not created in the classroom. Another factor that adds to the description of the problem is that the Department of Education, during the past decades, kept a policy of indifference towards the teaching of English... At the level between first and third grade, practically no English was taught (Puerto Rico Department of Education, 1997:12–13).

The policy belonged to the larger public policy of the PNP to translate its solid electoral support of the 1990s into a mandate for statehood. In 1993 it reestablished English as one of the two official languages of Puerto Rico. It had become clear during several congressional hearings in the 1980s that the proposition of statehood for Puerto Rico would arouse a strong opposition from English-only groups and their allies. Some critics of the PNP argue that it never truly pursued statehood, but rather used it as an excuse to funnel large sums of money that went to campaign finance funds and private enrichment. In fact, it ended in January 2001 when their rival PPD assumed power. The funds for English programs were reduced and the emphasis on the bilingual schools decreased. The policy suffered its final blow after the conviction in 2002 of former secretary Fajardo for corruption with several millions in funds from the department when he was in office.

Towards a New Paradigm: 2001 to the Present

The return of the PPD to power represented the end of the Fajardo policy. The Puerto Rican senate held public hearings and published a report on the language issue that concluded unambiguously in favor of Spanish as the sole official language:

> The Spanish tongue must be the only official language of Puerto Rico for the purpose of its domestic government affairs (Committee on Education, Science and Culture of the Senate of Puerto Rico, 2004: 131).

However, Governor Sila Calderón (2001–2004) refused to even discuss the possibility of legislating against the use of English. The education department under Secretary César Rey (2001–2004), quietly reinstated the English educational use to its condition before Fajardo. Rey was a *Hostosiano*, a follower of the pedagogical ideas of Eugenio María de Hostos, a nineteenth century educator and independence supporter. Rey stressed the teaching of Spanish and became a language stakeholder in its favor. His policy reduced the use of English as a medium of instruction but did not eliminate it. So, while Calderon's public discourse stressed the importance of learning English as an agent of social mobility, the department reduced its educational role once again. After Rey's departure, an interim secretary was named, Gloria Baquero. Her nomination did not get enough votes for confirmation in the Puerto Rican senate, apparently because she attempted to exercise the department's autonomy by refusing to employ people for political favors.

Baquero's successor, Rafael Aragunde (2005–2008), followed Rey's educational language policy. His tenure was marked by a confrontation with the *Federación de Maestros de Puerto Rico*. The confrontation ended with the decertification of the union as the representation of the teachers with the employer. However, they did not argue over Aragunde's language policy. In 2007, the department of education did not obtain a grant from the Reading First program for the teaching of Spanish because it refused to apply a methodology designed to teach English.

The next political shift in 2008 brought the pro-statehood coalition back to power, with the largest electoral advantage in over 40 years.

Governor Luis Fortuño's administration, however, prioritized the state of the economy. The educational language policy did not play a large role until the last year of his tenure in 2012, an election year. His first secretary of education, Odette Piñeiro (2009) stayed in the post for a few months and did not get a chance to implement a new educational language policy . Her replacement, Jesús Rivera Sánchez (2009–2011) stayed longer and implemented a program for teachers' capacitation in conjunction with the University of Puerto Rico that came under fire for the politization and irregularities in its implementation. Rivera continued with the practice of creating sporadic bilingual schools, but without changing the curriculum in the rest. In 2012, Fortuño announced a plan to increase the number of bilingual schools at a steady rate each year until it converted most public schools to an all-English curriculum. The new secretary, Eduard Moreno (2012), implemented the plan and instituted English summer camps for teachers and students. This renewed emphasis, however, seemed to respond more to an electoral strategy during an election year than to a real change in educational language policy. Fortuño lost the November 2012 elections to PPD's Alejandro García Padilla, who named Rafael Román as secretary of education in 2013. The official website of the department of education announced in June 2013 that:

> Schools will continue to be transformed, where teachers can receive the opportunities and tools to prepare bilingual students and for a globalized world. (http://www.de.gobierno.pr/secretario-del-de-defiende-presupuesto-de-3609-billones).

However, there have been no circular letters referring specifically to the bilingual schools or to the English question. If the pro-statehood makes any progress during Governor García Padilla's administration, it is likely that he will become a pro-Spanish language stakeholder.

---

[1] The curriculum organization was a straight application of Massachusetts' school curriculum, and the texts offered little sensibility towards Puerto Rican cultural idiosyncrasies. This fact was recognized by Falkner, who noted as an example how a school text illustrated a mathematical problem with peaches, which were unknown to most Puerto Rican children at the time, when it would have made more sense to illustrate it with a familiar fruit, like bananas (in Negrón de Montilla, 1990:110).

[2] The *Partido Socialista Obrero* did not support a Marxist or social democratic ideology, in spite of its name.

5
Uses of English in Puerto Rico

The conflict around the English question in Puerto Rico emerged from the state's attempts to manipulate the social use of the language by modifying its educational use. It shows the power of education as an agent of social change.

The social presence of English in Puerto Rico is often underestimated, probably because it is compared to that of Spanish. However, a better comparison would be with French, Dutch or any other language spoken in the Caribbean. While a person in Puerto Rico may spend a whole life without ever using French, he will need at least a basic knowledge of English. Outside of schools, English is present on television, internet, radio, business names, instruction labels, medical prescriptions, movie theaters, auto parts, and many other areas of daily life. English occupies a prominent role in Puerto Rican society that no other second or foreign language can challenge. This chapter is about its growth in Puerto Rican society.

English Social Use

The social use of English in Puerto Rico at the turn of the twentieth century began as a tertiary language with secondary elements, according to Figure 5.1. It experienced a rapid and steady growth every decade until it attained the level of a secondary language during the 1930s. By the 1950s the social use of English in Puerto Rico had increased to the level of a secondary language with primary elements. It continued decreasing its rate of growth until the present when it seems to have reached a plateau that may last a few more decades.

This model presents a general picture of language use in Puerto Rico from a macro societal perspective. It does not deny the variations in the intensity and variety of English according to region, socioeconomic status, and migration patterns. From a diachronic perspective, those variations in linguistic habits have reflected issues like waves of migration, changes in colonial policies, penetration of the American media, and economic development strategies. For instance, the 2000 census reported that the 10 municipalities with the highest levels of English knowledge in Puerto Rico were all located on the Northeast and East coasts. The census also showed that there were small pockets of competent English speakers around the island (Pousada, 2010:5). Some of those enclaves were created by Puerto Rican return migrants from the United States; others resulted from American immigrants. While they are relatively small when taken individually, at the aggregate level they become noticeable.

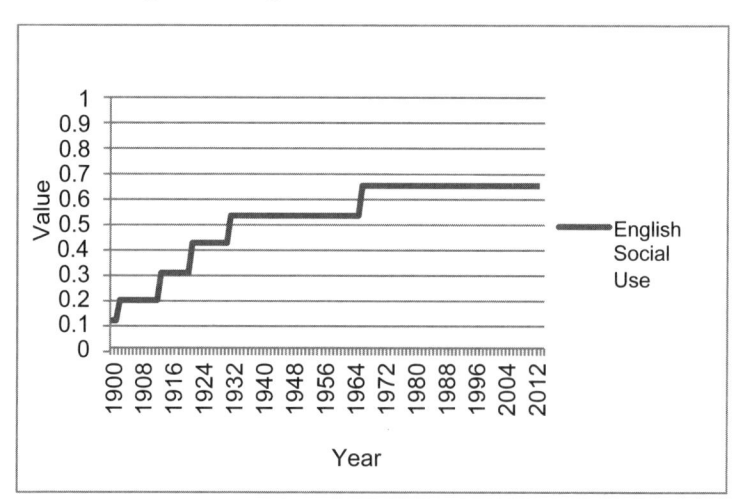

Figure 5.1 English Social Use in Puerto Rico

English Social Use during the Americanization Policy, 1898–1916

During the first decade of the twentieth century, few people were competent English speakers in Puerto Rico. Among those who spoke the language fluently, there were American government officials, soldiers, and Puerto Ricans who interacted with them. For instance, department heads, such as the commissioner of health or the auditor were imported from the United States and spoke no Spanish, so their communications within and outside their offices had to be conducted in English. This required the hiring of competent English speakers. It also meant that many Spanish speaking public employees were expected to use some English at work. These people represented a small percentage of the population and few used English at home. Also, Washington created a federal district court in Puerto Rico, postal offices, customs bureaus, and other agencies where English was used extensively.

In terms of legal status, the Official Languages Act of 1902 established both English and Spanish as official languages for government communications and activities (Morris, 1996:19). Government transactions were conducted in Spanish and English, but given the preponderance of English speakers in the executive council (the governor's cabinet and upper legislative branch) and executive branch, a large share of transactions were conducted in English.

At the turn of the century, English played a small social role in Puerto Rico. The 1900 census showed that only 3.6 percent of the population claimed to speak English, and the language had no official status. Table 2.1 indicates that English had a social use of a tertiary language:

$$(0.13)(0.90) + (0)(0.10) = 0.12$$

After the Official Languages Act of 1902 the social use of English increased to a tertiary language with secondary elements. Census data for 1900 showed that 3.6 percent of the population could speak English, while its legal status was one of several official languages.

The new value for English socialuse use is:

$$(0.13)(0.90) + (0.80)(0.10) = 0.20$$

The English social role was tertiary because of its minimal function as a tool of mass communication and little relevance for the job market, in spite of its growing role in government operations. Most people had no use for English except for teachers and government administrators at medium and high levels. The secondary elements were produced by its legal status as an official language, which legitimized its disproportionately large use in government operations. A tertiary role with secondary elements by no means implies an insignificant role, and that English played a role *at all* in Puerto Rican society was a considerable development. The rapid growth in social relevance by English was baffling if one considers that seven years earlier English use in the island was almost null, and that most individuals who were educated abroad did so in Europe and learned French, rather than English, as a second language. The fact that education commissioners were eventually disappointed with their policies' failures testifies to their wide reaching goals, which did not allow them to realize the true and noteworthy effects of their practices. In fact, they helped establish a social presence for English in less than 20 years, which is fast for a change in linguistic habits.

For most members of the Puerto Rican political elite it was apparent that the sovereignty of the U.S. over Puerto Rico would be a long term affair, and that knowledge of English would become an important skill. In fact, most arguments against the preferential treatment of English did not propose its elimination, but rather a reduction on emphasis and the eradication of the Americanization philosophy behind its use. The arguments essentially exposed the problems produced by the educational language gap. An article published in *La Educación Moderna* by Ana Roqué, a Puerto Rican teacher, argued that:

> It has been a mistake to trust young children to American teachers... Personally I consider inevitable to have knowledge of English... but with the means and methods used in our schools to teach it, I consider it inhuman, incorrect, and upsetting (in Negrón de Montilla, 1990:119).

For this distinguished teacher, using the current methods was "inhuman," but learning English was "inevitable." The issue was not whether to teach English, but to what extent.

English Social Use during the Second Phase of the Americanization Policy, 1916–1934

There were several changes in the social role of English in the two decades after the establishment of Falkner's policy. The biggest change was a strong increase in the number of people who spoke English, with a growth of 175 percent between 1910 and 1920, according to population censuses. The number of speakers was low (3.6 percent of the population in 1910 and 9.9 percent in 1920), but the growth rate was large. This increase was mainly motivated by a combination of the language policy and an intensification of U.S. economic penetration in the island, which brought monolingual English speakers as entrepreneurs, technocrats, managers, and civil servants. On the government level, there was a decline in the use of English, due to the creation of an elective senate with the Jones Act of 1917. The senate became dominated by Puerto Rican politicians who performed the body's functions in Spanish. Since the senate replaced the executive council, which conducted their business in English, the relative volume of government transactions held in English declined. The use of English at official levels was still high, since the governor and several cabinet members were Americans who either spoke no Spanish or preferred to speak English. Also, the judges of the supreme court of Puerto Rico were appointed by the U.S. president. Overall, the value for English social use was higher in 1916 (Miller/Huyke policy) than in 1904 (Falkner policy), due to the increase in English speakers and the growth in U.S. economic penetration.

The increase in the number of people that reported to know English in the 1920 census to 9.9 percent produced a new value in the social use as follows:

$$(0.25)(0.9) + (0.80)(0.10) = 0.31$$

The value of 0.31 places the English use during this period as that of a secondary language. This change from a tertiary language with secondary elements to a secondary language represented a significant increase in a relatively short period. It shows how deep the strategy had penetrated and how the U.S. presence was quickly transforming Puerto Rican society.

The 1930s saw an increase in the English social use index due to a rise in the number of people who claimed to speak English. The increase also showed the effects of several decades of persecution by the American and Puerto Rican governments against those who opposed the assimilationist policies (Bosque-Pérez, 2003:14). By then the Americanization policy had affected two generations of Puerto Rican school children and it had begun to bear fruits. The educational language policy established in 1934 would deal with that new reality.

English Social Use and the Decline of the Americanization Policy, 1934–1948

When Padín assumed the leadership of the department in 1930, the population census data showed an increase from 9.9 percent in 1920 to 19.4 percent in 1930. The change represented a 96 percent increase in 10 years, slightly lower than the previous decade, but still large. The increase resulted from a continuation of the same dynamics that had induced a growth in English social use before: increased economic penetration by the United States, particularly through direct capital investments in agriculture, and the continued effects of the emphasis on English instruction in the public school system. The use of English in government remained high, since many government posts were still occupied by English speakers, particularly in the executive and the judiciary. World War II produced an increase in the federal presence after the building of several military bases, particularly Ramey and Roosevelt Roads. They became the center of the offensive against the U-boats in the Caribbean Sea, where the Germans sunk over 300 merchant ships that brought raw materials and foodstuffs from Latin America to Europe and Northern Africa.

The application of the English social use indicators for 1930 places the value of 19.4 percent within the range of 10 to 20 percent, while its official role remained as that of one of two official languages. It indicates a growth in the social use of English:

$$(0.38)(0.90) + (0.80)(0.10) = 0.42$$

The value of 0.42 indicates that English remained a secondary language, but with an obvious increase in its relative role. It is clear that, arguments against notwithstanding, the role of English in Puerto Rican society increased steadily since 1900.

The Puerto Rican society was still largely divided between two major positions regarding the English question. The underlying difference resided in their understanding of the desired social role of English in Puerto Rican society. Those who believed in the need to establish English as a primary language because of the political and economic ties with the U.S. supported a primary role in education. This group included supporters of Puerto Rico's inclusion into the American Union, the *Partido Republicano*, the *Partido Socialista Obrero*, a fraction of the *Partido Unión*, and most American colonial administrators. On the other hand, the groups that believed that English should receive the attention of a tertiary or foreign language opposed its use as an instructional medium. This group consisted mostly of autonomists, separatists, most of the *Partido Unión*, and many teachers who bore the brunt of the weight to enforce the various language policies. Language stakeholders involved in the long debate on the language question based their theoretical justifications on either interpretation of English's social role in Puerto Rican society. Thus, all educational language policies were ultimately justified by education commissioners in terms of their correspondence with the language's expected or real social role. For instance, Padín specified that:

> The general objective (of his new policy was) to give pupils such a working knowledge of English as may be justified by their social and vocational needs (Circular Letter 39, 1934).

It becomes clear that the debate over the educational role of English can improve with a standard methodology to measure the language's social role and understand its changes through time. The social use categories introduced in this book perform such a task.

By 1935, the population census indicated a growth in English knowledge to 22.9 percent of the population. This new data changed its social use as follows:

$$(0.50)(0.90) + (0.80)(0.10) = 0.53$$

The value of 0.53 reveals that English had become a secondary language with primary elements. It has stayed in that position until today, while Spanish has retained its undisputed primary role. Puerto Rican society had embarked on the long and tortuous road towards bilingualism, in spite of predictions to the contrary by opponents of the Americanization tactics. This is not to say that most Puerto Ricans were becoming bilingual, but rather that English was gradually increasing and infusing bilingual characteristics to Puerto Rican society. Language diversity had become part of the Puerto Rican identity. That diversity increased during the following decades with the mass migration to the U.S. and the emergence of thousands of Anglophone Puerto Ricans, many of whom would return in the 1970s.

English Social Use and the Puertoricanization Policy, 1949–1969

The social role of English between 1949 and 1969 experienced an increase on some aspects and a decrease in others. The use of English as a medium of instruction during the preceding decades had produced various generations of Puerto Ricans who had been exposed to an intense English education. Even after the process came to an end after the elimination of English as a language of instruction in 1949 it became evident that the decades of Americanization policies took roots. The economic front also produced an increase in the role of English by boosting the direct capital investment of U.S. manufacturing corporations and creating many jobs that required the use of English, which enhanced the general perception that English was the language of social mobility and economic progress. However, English use in government affairs was drastically reduced by the Puertoricanization of the bureaucracy produced by the popular election of the governor and the end of the practice of U.S. presidents to name some of the governor's cabinet members. The replacement of English monolingual bureaucrats by Spanish speakers reduced the role of English in government operations. Finally and most importantly, the Puertoricanization of education ended the disproportionate emphasis on English instruction.

Census data shows that by 1949, 26.1 percent of the population claimed to know English. The social use of English during that period remained a secondary language with primary elements:

$$(0.50)(0.90) + (0.80)(0.10) = 0.53$$

The 1960 census reveals an increase in English knowledge to 37.7 percent. The application of Table 2.1 shows a similar value for that of 1949, so the social use of English in Puerto Rico remained as that of a secondary language with primary elements. It is significant that the populist government of Muñoz Marín which relied so heavily on the symbols of cultural nationalism, did not strip English of its official status granted by the Official Languages Act of 1902.

Puerto Rico experienced a rapid modernization process between 1950 and 1970. The country became industrialized with an increase in manufacture's share of the GDP from 15 percent in 1950 to 26 percent in 1970 (Irizarry-Mora, 2011:124). The cities swelled and the countryside shrunk. Agriculture's share of GDP fell from 18 percent in 1950 to 3 percent in 1970 (Irizarry-Mora, 2011:122). American multinational corporations became the almost exclusive form of industrial capital investment. Also, thousands of Puerto Ricans migrated to the United States and new social forces emerged that changed the debate over English in Puerto Rican society.

English Social Use and the Bilingualization Policy, 1969–present

The English social use in Puerto Rico continued to grow, but at slower rates than in preceding decades. The growth rate was reaching a plateau that would stabilize in the 1990s. Many first and second generation Puerto Ricans who had migrated during the 1950s and 1960s returned to the island to stay. At the same time, many Puerto Ricans continued to migrate to the United States, some to relocate and others to study in American universities. The result was what some have called the air bus, a continuing flow of outward and inward migration of thousands of people every year. Many of the returning migrants spoke mainly English or Spanglish, and little or no Spanish, while many of those who came back from U.S. universities changed their linguistic habits to include large doses of English in their daily use. Secretary Benítez stressed the importance of the return migration, stating that:

The growing number of foreign students and from the United States that apply for admission into the country's private and public schools requires our most careful attention, so these students can become integrated to their new education situation in a quick and efficient manner. Given that the largest number of applications comes from students transferred from the city of New York, I wish to have your cooperation so that every month the Principals from private and public schools fill out and send to the regional Director the Monthly Report of Pupils Admitted from New York City (Circular Letter 34, 1973).

Also, the appearance of cable television during the 1970s introduced Puerto Ricans to hundreds of English-speaking channels. Hence, for a growing segment of the population, English played a significant role.

The language social use increased in 1970, but the language category index reveals that it remained a secondary language with primary elements. The 1970 census showed that 42.7 percent of the population claimed to know English, thus:

$$(0.63)(0.90) + (0.80)(0.10) = 0.65$$

By 1980 the value remained essentially intact, even with a slight increase in census data showing English usage to 45.6 percent, which produced a value of 0.65. The 1990 census showed another increase to 50.5 percent of the population reporting to speak English. In the 20 years between 1970 and 1990, English usage had increased by 18 percent. Nevertheless, English remained a secondary language with primary elements.

A considerable, but short lasting change, occurred in the social use index of English in 1991. Hernández Colón replaced the 90-year-old Official Languages Act by a new law that established Spanish as the sole official language of Puerto Rico. The new value for social use became:

$$(0.63)(0.90) + (0.00)(0.10) = 0.57$$

The social use index for English decreased, but it remained a secondary language with primary elements. English became an official language again in 1993, so its social use returned to 0.65.

The social use of English has reached a stability that seems unlikely to change at the short or medium term because of the stagnant rate of growth of English speakers in Puerto Rico. Given its current value as a secondary language with primary elements, it would need an annual 20 percent rate of increase to reach the next level of a primary language in the near future. There are no indications that it will grow at such a rate.

English Educational Use in Puerto Rico

English had no educational use in Puerto Rico until its introduction as a secondary language in 1899. Figure 5.2 reveals that it reached its highest levels between 1908 and 1916, when it became a primary language in the public school system. English was the only medium of instruction; teachers were required to show proficiency in it, students were expected to speak it even during recess, and Spanish courses were eliminated for the early grades. However, the pattern after 1916 was one of constant reduction until it reached the minimal role of a tertiary language in 1949. The value remained constant until 1969, when English increased its educational role to that of a tertiary language with secondary elements. After that it experienced an increase, reaching its highest level during the late 1990s when it briefly became a secondary language with primary elements. It currently occupies the role of a tertiary language with secondary elements.

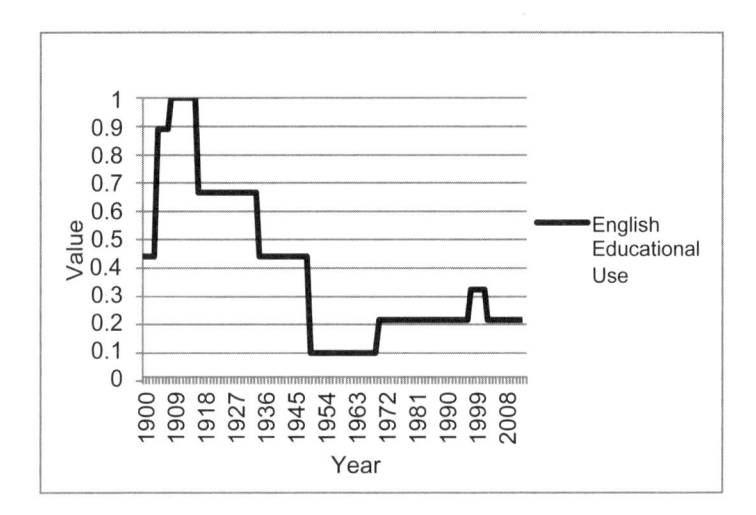

Figure 5.2 English Educational Use in Puerto Rico

English Educational Use and the Americanization Policy, 1898–1916

The education of Puerto Ricans was a salient issue for the American colonial administrators. The military government that ruled the island from 1898 to 1900 created many institutions and practices that survived well into the twentieth century. The Americanization policy rested on three pillars: the use of English as a medium of instruction, the teaching of English as a language course, and the hiring of native English speakers. It followed Richard Henry Pratt's motto of "kill the Indian, save the man" (in Rosa, 2003). General Nelson Miles, who led the 1898 invasion of Puerto Rico, and John Eaton, who created the public educational system in Puerto Rico, were key figures in the federal handling of the Native American populations in the U.S. at the end of the 1800s. They imbued the same racist philosophy into Puerto Rican political and educational institutions.

The new policy established English as the instructional medium from eighth grade, with a daily English language course from first grade. It increased its role.

$$(0.38)(0.90) + (1.00)(0.10) = 0.44$$

This value of 0.44 places the educational use of English in 1900 as a secondary language. The English course itself was taught as a first language, even though most children had never spoken it.

Brumbaugh maintained the educational use of English as a secondary language, and intensified the practice of hiring American teachers. Falkner and Dexter established the most aggressive Americanization practices in Puerto Rican history. They attempted a radical transculturation of the Puerto Rican population into American language and cultural habits. However, this does not mean that colonial administrators believed that by being Americanized, Puerto Ricans would become Americans. The American identity was defined as that of white protestant English speakers who descended from Northern Europeans (Schildkraut, 2003). Puerto Ricans were colored catholic Spanish speakers who descended from Southern Europeans and Africans. They would never fit the mold, but could become loyal to American ideals. American officials tried to assimilate a people they believed inferior. Victor Clark, President of the Insular Board of Education in 1899, had stated that:

> The great masses of Puerto Ricans are as yet passive and plastic . . . Their ideals are in our hands to create and mold (in Morris, 1995:26).

Falkner's policy continued the teaching of English courses from first grade, a practice established during the Eaton/Clark transitional phase from the Spanish to the American system. However, in 1905 English was upgraded from a special subject in schools, to the primary language of instruction, beginning in second grade, while it continued to be taught as a language course in all grades. The change produced the following value:

$$(0.88)(0.90) + (1.00)(0.10) = 0.89$$

Falkner has come to symbolize the worse of the Americanization policies. The value of 0.89 classifies the educational use of English in 1904 as that of a primary language. Dexter, his replacement, intensified even more the use of English as a medium of instruction, starting it in first grade since 1908:

$$(1.00)(0.90) + (1.00)(0.10) = 1.00$$

The value of 1.00 classifies the teaching of English as a primary language. Puerto Rican children were educated in an intense immersion program with little support from their community where English was rarely spoken. This was the peak of the Americanization policy. Not only was English upgraded, but Spanish was reduced to a minimal use. Spanish was not taught in first grade, and limited to one class period starting on second grade. The difficulties with the policy were evident from the onset, especially for rural schools, which were harder to access, had fewer resources, and represented a second choice for most teachers. It was also clear from reports, circular letters, and writings, that children weren't adopting the American culture, language, and values at the expected rate. Falkner, in a circular letter to the department's superintendents, argued that:

> The rapid and widespread increase in grade teaching in English is the most noteworthy recent development in our work. In many places, however, the results have not been such as were hoped for. Among the causes which have contributed to make work unsatisfactory are the placing of inexperienced American teachers in charge of grades they could not control, the frequent changes in American teachers, carrying on English grade work in towns where adequate supervision was impossible, putting high grades in charge of Porto Rican teachers who could not successfully teach them in English, and lack of comprehension of the difficulties of the work on the part of teachers and superintendents (Circular Letter 421, 1907).

Falkner realized the lack of success of his language policy in replacing Spanish for English, but did not mention among its causes the difficulties in changing the language habits of an entire population and the resilience of Spanish as a means of mass communication in Puerto Rico. In fact, the attempt to establish English as the primary language of Puerto Ricans was partly based on a belief that the large numbers of illiterates in Puerto Rico would permit the substitution of one language pattern by another. It was also based in the qualification of the Puerto Rican variety as a second-rate Spanish, in clear diglossic terms. Victor Clark, President of the Puerto Rico Education Board between 1899 and 1900, in a widely quoted statement declared that:

> There does not seem to be among the (Puerto Rican) masses the same devotion to their native tongue or to any national ideal that animate the frenchman for instance, in Canada or the Rhine provinces. Another important fact that must not be overlooked is that a majority of the people of this island do not speak pure Spanish. The language is a patois almost unintelligible to the natives of Barcelona and Madrid. It possesses no literature and little value as an intellectual medium. There is a bare possibility that it will be nearly as easy to educate this people out of their patois into English as it will be to educate them into the elegant tongue of Castile (Cebollero, 1945:6).

Thirty years later, long after out of office, Clark still believed that:

> English is the chief source, practically the only source, of democratic ideas in Porto Rico. There may be little that they learn to remember, but the English school reader itself provides a body of ideas and concepts which are not to be had in any other way (Clark, 1930:81).

This underestimation of the stability and richness of four hundred years of Spanish use in the island led several education commissioners to believe in the feasibility of establishing English as the instructional medium in Puerto Rican schools.

Even those who did not share Clark's contempt towards Puerto Rican culture believed it possible to establish a primary social role for English in Puerto Rico. Brumbaugh, six years after resigning his post, expressed:

> The first business of the American republic, in its attempt to universalize its educational ideals in America, is to give these Spanish-speaking races the symbols of the English language in which to express knowledge and the culture which they already possess... Another matter is that, while these people are acquiring thus the

symbols of a new language, they must not be allowed to neglect the perfecting of their thought in the symbols of their native tongue... This was demonstrated in our experience in Porto Rico, and it would be a great injustice to the Spanish-American civilization to undertake to remove the language of their native country, so rich in literature, so glorious in history (Brumbaugh, 1907:65).

In spite of the large obstacles faced by the implementation of the policy, and against its meager results relative to its ambitious goals, the English educational policy remained virtually intact during eleven years. English was used as the medium of instruction from second (and eventually first) grade, English courses were mandatory from first grade, and teaching licenses required knowledge of English.

English Educational Use during the Second Phase of the Americanization Policy, 1916–1934

Miller's new policy in 1916 reduced the intensity of English educational use. School children would receive instruction in Spanish until the fourth grade, with fifth grade serving as a transition to an all-English curriculum after sixth grade. For rural schools, where most children left school before sixth grade, the real implications of the new policy were that the majority received their education in Spanish, except for English language courses. For graded (urban) schools, the new policy implied Spanish instruction for most of their elementary school (López Yustos, 1997:132).

The application of Table 2.1 for 1916 reveals a considerable decrease in the educational role of English:

$$(0.63)(0.90) + (1.00)(0.10) = 0.67$$

The educational use of English was reduced from 1.00 in 1908 to 0.67 in 1916; from a primary language to a secondary language with primary elements. This change represented a moderation of the Americanization policy, although the objectives remained unscathed. In a letter addressed to school supervisors, Miller explained:

> The elimination of English reading in the first and second grades is in no way to be construed as a change of attitude by the Department as to the advisability of teaching English. Children will receive a thorough drill in the elements of Spanish before making a study of the mechanics of English reading. Beginning with the third grade, however, children will learn to read in English and thereafter teachers

are reminded that the aim is to make children bilingual. The slogan of the school is 'The conservation of Spanish and the acquisition of English' (Circular Letter 18, 1917).

Huyke also supported the Americanization policy, believed in the progressive nature of American ideals and cultural norms, and insisted on instilling those values through the public school system. For instance, the education department sponsored the American Education Week in conjunction with the National Education Association of America and the American Legion. For such objective, he stated that:

> The main purpose of the week is to inform the public of the accomplishments and needs of the public schools to secure cooperation and support in meeting these needs and to teach and foster good Americanism... The following topics are suggested for use in schools: Monday, Our Flag; Tuesday, American Ideals; Wednesday, The Language of America; Thursday, Emigration; Friday, Illiteracy... Patriotic music should be sung and played and the meaning of the American Flag taught and the flag honored. Members of the American Legion and others should be invited to speak at meetings in the schools and in the community (Circular Letter 59, 1921).

His vision about the desired effect of his educational policy on the social use of English was similar to Miller's: Puerto Ricans should become bilingual, and the public school system was the means to achieve it. He wrote to school supervisors and special teachers of English:

> Under the present conditions, however, as the use of English is becoming more of a necessity in our everyday life, the position of this Special Teacher of English in each locality seems to point to the fact that the scope of her activities should include specifically the promotion of the wider use of English, particularly spoken English, not only in the school or system of schools in which she works, but in so far as possible, in the community itself (Circular Letter 78, 1928).

In order to encourage a more widespread use of English, Huyke requested the creation of English Clubs for students and teachers, Young People's English Clubs (for community members outside the schools), contests, English libraries, publications in English by teachers, the use of English by pupils among themselves during recess, and evening classes for adults. He also established an oral English exam as a high school graduation requirement in 1922, which was rejected by the AMPR on the grounds that it was too difficult. The meager test results seemed to confirm the association's concerns. For instance, in 1924, the average score on the exam was 46 percent, or a 1.85 out of a maximum 4 points score (Circular Letter 192, 1924). The policy continued in place until 1934.

English Educational Use during the Decline of the Americanization Policy, 1934–1948

Padín was no stranger to the debate about English instruction. Besides publishing an influential study, he wrote frequently in domestic newspapers and magazines. The reduction on the emphasis in English stemmed from a fundamental difference in his perception of English's social role in Puerto Rican society relative to the previous education commissioners. He saw the role of English as that of a foreign tongue with an important presence in Puerto Rican society, a departure from the view of English as a primary language.

In the United States, the Americanization policy and persecution of immigrants had toned down, while many English proficiency requirements were removed (Crawford, 1990). While not actively pursuing minority linguistic rights, the federal government allowed more leeway to individual states and territories.

Padín considered English to be a foreign language, contrary to all previous education commissioners. Pedro Cebollero, assistant commissioner of education under his administration, pointed out that "it is inconceivable that they (education commissioners) should have admitted that English was a foreign language and that they should have insisted on its use as the vehicle of instruction" (1945:23). For instance, Miller shifted the emphasis on first grade English from reading to conversation and argued that it "brought the Porto Rican child a step nearer to the level of the American child who hears and talks English four or five years before he is required to read it" (Miller, 1917:464). The comparison between Puerto Rican and American children evidenced Miller's intentions to bring the former's knowledge of the language to the level of the latter, for which English was a primary language. The emphasis on English use outside the classroom, including the playground, was based on a desire to turn English into a primary language as well. Padín, in turn, established a distinction between Spanish as the mother tongue and English as a second language, and his policy reflected that distinction. Thus, he argued that "English can be taught effectively, without displacing or corrupting the mother tongue" (Padín, 1935:1).

The 1934 language policy reduced the use of English as the instructional medium to grades eight through twelve, and modified the approach of teaching English as a subject. Until then, English texts were designed for native speakers who used the language at home and brought a previous knowledge of it to the classroom (Cebollero, 1945). For example, language exercises emphasized the prevention and correction of mistakes typical of native English speakers. However, Puerto Rican children displayed other types of mistakes, typical of learners of a second or foreign language. Padín's policy adapted the teaching of English to that of a second language, reducing its role as an instructional medium while modifying its role as a language subject. For the latter purpose, he increased the daily time allotted for English as a subject. In this sense, he did not intend to eliminate the use of English, but rather to adapt it to what he perceived to be its role. In spite of the *Republicanos'* and *Socialistas'* accusations to the contrary, he expressed strong pro-American views, and subscribed to the idea of tightening the cultural bonds with the United States.

The numerical representation reveals an educational use of a secondary language. It represented a return to 1900 levels:

$$(0.38)(0.90) + (1.00)(0.10) = 0.44$$

An important criterion in selecting Gallardo, Padín's replacement, was his view on the language question. Roosevelt's pressure provoked him to modify the educational language policy. While Roosevelt did not refer to any specific policy changes, it was clear that he was reacting against Padín's reduction in English use. Thus, Gallardo wasted no time in reforming the existing policy and announced his new plan at a general meeting with the superintendents of schools in 1937 (Osuna, 1949:377). The main goal of his plan can be summarized in his own words:

> Our chief objective in the teaching of English has been the intensifying of the work sufficiently to enable us to attain a workable bilingual program of education (Gallardo, 1938:16).

In five years, however, the unclear nature of his policies, coupled with the adverse reaction by the AMPR and large sectors of the public, made him return to his predecessor's practices. After reversing his experimental changes, his motives were questioned and criticized by Washington officials, particularly the secretary of the interior Harold L. Ickes (Osuna, 1949:387; López Yustos, 1997:164). Gallardo, deposing in front of the Subcommittee of the Committee on Territories and Insular Affairs, defended his position:

> We make efforts to teach English. We teach it through the elementary schools and in the high schools. However, the only opportunities for the use of English afforded to a child in Puerto Rico are exclusively those of the school. Teaching English is seriously handicapped by the environment, which is Spanish. The biggest mistake made by anyone is to think that we can achieve bilingualism. In Puerto Rico it is impossible to obtain a situation where our people will master both languages equally well (in Osuna, 1949:385).

Gallardo's experiment, quickly reversed, did not constitute a new policy.

English Educational Use during the Puertoricanization Policy, 1949–1969

Villaronga replaced Gallardo and swiftly ended the Americanization educational policy with circular letter number 10. It established the foundations of the educational language policy that would remain in effect for decades. It completely erased the role of English as a medium of instruction but kept it as a language course for all grades. Right before the new policy, English was the medium of instruction since high school, while Spanish was the medium of instruction for grammar and middle schools. He changed that when he declared that:

> According to announcements on previous occasions, Spanish will be the medium of instruction in high school. This change, which responds to a necessity felt through several years, extends definitely the use of the vernacular as the medium of instruction until the last year of high school (Circular Letter 10, 1949).

The issue went virtually unnoticed in Washington, where the perceived threat over the American way of life shifted from immigration to communism. The value for the educational use of English in 1949 decreased dramatically from previous years:

$$(0.00)(0.90) + (1.00)(0.10) = 0.10$$

The value of 0.10 placed English in the category of a tertiary language. English ceased to be used as a medium of instruction until the end of the 1960s when new winds took over the government and the public education system.

Villaronga's successors as secretaries of public instruction (the new title after 1952), Sánchez Hidalgo, Oliveras and Quintero, maintained the educational language policy, each with its own twist. Particularly salient was Quintero's tenure because of his innovative pedagogical approaches. Also during his tenure there was a significant increase in U.S. grants towards education. Eventually this created a dependence on federal funds that affected the programmatic preferences of the school system. By 1969, one fifth of the department's funds came from federal grants. Beginning in the1970s, many of the goals established by the department of public instruction were chosen because they could receive grants and not for philosophical reasons.

English Educational Use and the Bilingualization Era, 1969–Present

The 1969 educational language policy reintroduced English as an instructional medium on a limited basis, essentially in bilingual education programs for returning migrants from the United States. Mellado's use of English as a medium of instruction classifies within the category "used as a medium of instruction for less than one fourth of all classes." As a language course, English kept its place for all grades. Then:

$$(0.13)(0.90) + (1.00)(0.10) = 0.22$$

The value of 0.22 indicates that the policy used English as a tertiary language with secondary elements, which was a significant increase in use from Villaronga's approach as a tertiary language.

The educational use of English was left intact until 1985 when Aponte Roque announced her intentions to establish a new policy eliminating the English language courses until the fourth grade and rescinding bilingual education programs. Had her changes been implemented, the educational use of English would have decreased in the following manner:

$$(0.00)(0.90) + (0.60)(0.10) = 0.06$$

Aponte Roque's policy would have moved the English educational use to that of a tertiary language. However, the public debates made clear that most people did not want English to occupy such a role. If anything, many people wanted the educational role of English to increase. The policy never took effect besides all the aggressive pro-Spanish rhetoric.

The next change in the English educational use came in 1997 with the implementation of Fajardo's policy. It reintroduced English as a medium of instruction for Science and Mathematics courses and increased the funds for the English program. The new value is:

$$(0.25)(0.90) + (1.00)(0.10) = 0.33$$

The policy increased qualitatively the ranking of English educational use to that of a secondary language. However, its effects could not be felt because of its short life as a policy, only from 1997 to 2000.

In 2001 secretary Rey (2001–2004) reverted Fajardo's policy and terminated the Bilingual Citizen Project. Rey returned the educational use of English to what it had been during Mellado's tenure. English as a medium of instruction was now reduced to less than one fourth of all classes, while it retained its place as a language course for all grades.

The new value became:

$$(0.13)(0.90) + (1.00)(0.10) = 0.22$$

Rey emphasized the role of Spanish underscoring a nationalist tone:

> The Spanish Program is the core that supports the goals and objectives of our Educational System. Spanish is our mother tongue. It is also the most relevant academic discipline because our language is the vehicle through which we communicate in each subject and in each learning instance (Circular Letter 23, 2004).

Aragunde continued with the pro-Spanish policy and argued that,

> Spanish, as the mother tongue, is the indispensable base in the Puerto Rican public school for the acquisition of knowledge in all academic areas and in the development of ethical, aesthetic, personal and social values. Besides being Spanish the base for all teaching, it is evident its functional importance as an instrument through which it is assured the social interaction and access to culture, base of the personal social and cultural changes typical of the dynamics of the current world (Circular Letter 1, 2008).

English is still used as a tertiary language with secondary elements, even after the return to power of the pro-statehood party in 2008. The new administration had been preoccupied with a declining economy, rising crime rates, and popular protests, so apparently it did not consider it politically reasonable to bring the issue back to the public debate, in spite of rhetoric to the contrary.

Finally in 2012, during their last year in office, Secretary Eduardo Moreno (2011–2012), who had attempted unsuccessfully to run for election as a house representative earlier, and Governor Fortuño surprised public opinion with the announcement of a new immersion experiment in public education. Public reactions echoed the past debates with the familiar language stakeholders jumping to the scene. The new policy barely took effect because Fortuño lost the election two months later and a new education secretary came to office.

Educational Language Gap

The story of the English ELAG in Puerto Rico is shown in Figure 5.3. It reached a peak in 1908 and a low in 1965. That is, in 1908, English was most overused, while in 1965 it was most underused. In 1934, the English ELAG approached zero, so the educational use of the language was close to its social use.

The peak in 1908 (0.80) reflects the most intense period of the Americanization policy in Puerto Rico. The low of 1965 (-0.55) represents the most intense period of the Puertoricanization policy. The transition period between both paradigms, 1934–1948, shows the smallest ELAG. The current value (-0.43) shows it is underused in the educational process.

Educational Language Gap, 1898–1916

The English ELAG emerged after 1899, when the new colonial administration established the educational institutions that brought about the Americanization policy. The values are determined by subtracting the social use from the educational use. The value is positive when the educational use is larger than the social use; the value is negative when the social use is higher than the educational use. It reaches cero when educational use and social use are similar. Between 1900 and 1916 the value for ELAG was always positive, ranging from 0.33 to 0.80. English was used initially as a secondary language but quickly jumped to that of a primary language. Its social use, however, remained that of a tertiary language with secondary elements (due to its official status).

The discrepancy between English social use and English educational use during the Americanization period sparkled several years of heated public debate. Falkner's policy created the basis for a diglossic situation in Puerto Rico, where English began to occupy the High functions of official and educational uses, while Spanish started to be relegated to the Low function of group communication. This diglossic tendency eventually became blurred by subsequent language policy changes that increased the role of Spanish in education and government use, but from then on English would at least share some of the High functions that were performed by Spanish until then. The policy also contributed to the perception that English provided better social mobility opportunities than Spanish, even if this perception was never empirically supported.

All three essential components of a diglossic situation were met in Puerto Rico:
a) English played the High function and evoked more prestige than Spanish;
b) Spanish occupied the Low function and was learned first, as a mother tongue, while English was learned later, mostly through schooling;
c) The dynamics between English and Spanish reflected the social and political relations between the speakers of either language (Ferguson, 1959; Fasold, 1987; Gumperz, 1964).

Most education policymakers acknowledged the eventual permanence of Spanish, but claimed that learning English would provide Puerto Rican children with a crucial tool for future social mobility. This social mobility was based on the belief that English was on its way to occupy the high social functions that provided the best employment opportunities and access to universal ideas and new technological knowledge. Miller conceived the issue in democratic terms, and believed that Puerto Rican children had the *right* to learn English through public education, since "as U.S. citizens, the children of Puerto Rico (had) the inalienable right to learn the English language" (in Negrón de Montilla, 1990:174).

In this sense education commissioners perceived their role as advancing progress to the island, since they viewed English as more prestigious and more useful for social mobility purposes. They reflected the racist view of the superiority of the white Americans over the dark races, supported by prejudiced scientific research that appealed to mainstream politics in the U.S. They were aware of the discrepancy between English social use and English educational use, but believed that their policies would reduce the gap. The year of 1908 shows the largest difference produced by Dexter's policies (see Figure 5.4).

Education commissioners were convinced that Puerto Ricans wanted to learn English, as Dexter expressed in a letter addressed to the American teachers:

> The people of Puerto Rico are anxious that their children learn the English language, and it is largely through you that the Department hopes to gratify their desire (Circular Letter 18, 1908).

The creation of a diglossic situation in Puerto Rico meant that those societal sectors that did not conform to the new linguistic situation paid a price in exclusion or in adaptation. Since the focus of the English language policy was the school system, the societal sectors affected initially and more strongly by the educational language gap were those involved in the educational process.

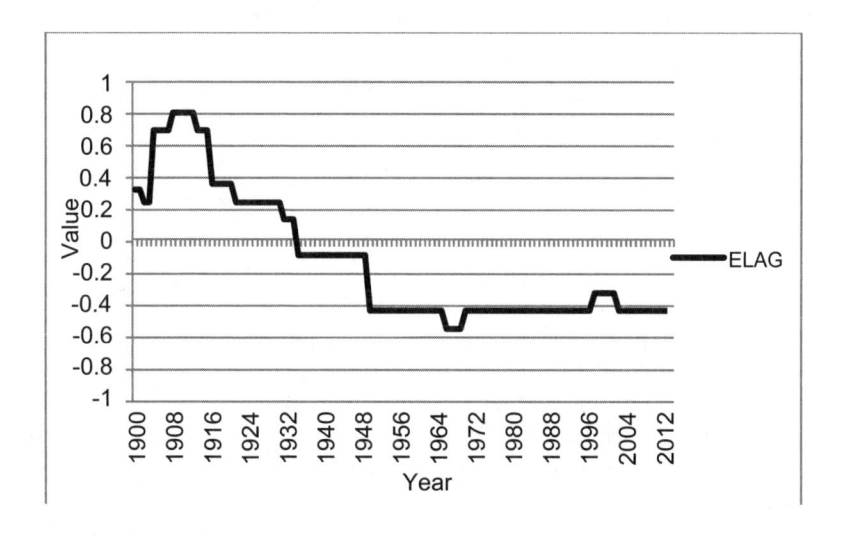

Figure 5.3: English ELAG in Puerto Rico

Educational Language Gap, 1916–1934

The English ELAG decreased during the Miller/Huyke policy period because both components of ELAG (social use and educational use) changed. The English social use increased, as shown by Figure 5.1. On the other hand, the new educational language policy reduced the emphasis on English, moving the educational use closer to the social use. The value of ELAG is based on a social use of English as secondary language, compared to its educational use as a secondary language with primary elements. The ELAG value for the period was 0.36, which meant an overuse of English similar to that of 1900.

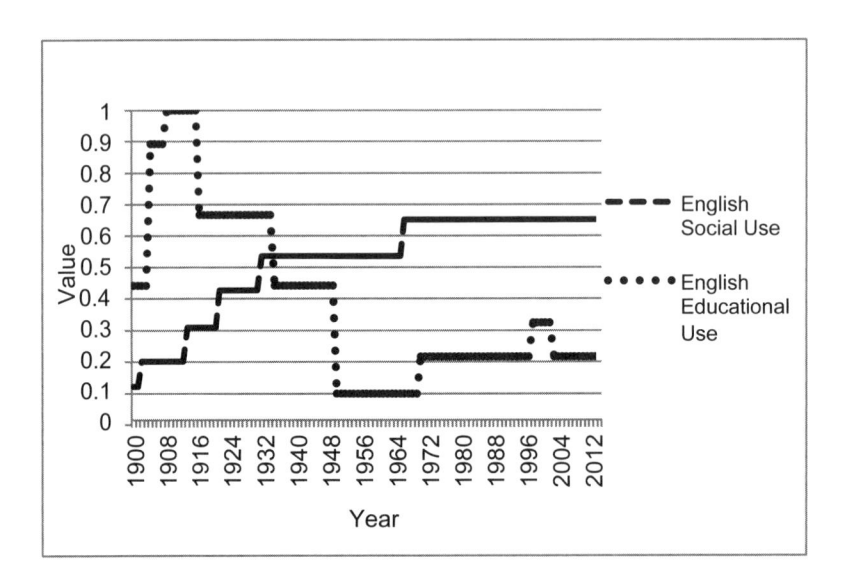

Figure 5.4 Uses of English in Puerto Rico

The diglossic situation continued, even with the reduction in government operations held in English. The U.S. economic presence continued to expand with the boom of sugar production in Puerto Rico. Most jobs created by U.S. sugar corporations opened in the manual labor areas, such as tilling and processing sugar cane. Management jobs required knowledge of English and, although most of them were occupied by imported English-speakers, the public perception that the higher posts required English reinforced the prestige of English as an agent of social mobility. That perception helped maintain the diglossic dynamics between English/High and Spanish/Low languages.

Educational Language Gap, 1934–1948

The trend in ELAG reduction persisted during the 1930s. Both components of ELAG experienced changes in values that brought them closer. By 1934, when the Padín policy was created, the English social use was that of a secondary language, which signified a considerable growth from the early years when English occupied the role of a tertiary language with secondary elements. Educational use, the other component of ELAG, decreased in value. In 1934 English educational use became that of a secondary language, also a departure from Miller's approach. The effect of changes in both components was a reduction in ELAG, reflecting a closer relationship between the use of English in education and its role in society. In fact, the years between 1934 and 1948 show the smallest ELAG of the twentieth century in Puerto Rico, reflecting the correspondence between the educational and social uses of English.

The policy reduced the diglossic relationship between English and Spanish in the area of education by decreasing the popular perception that the former was a better language for the transmission of progressive concepts than the latter. This was an important development because one of the bases for diglossia is the perception that a High language is better suited than a Low language for the learning of dynamic ideas and knowledge (Ferguson, 1959). The policy supported the perception that Spanish could transmit modern universal values derived from a rich cultural heritage. However, the increased economic dependence on the United States, which intensified during the critical 1930s, helped sustain the belief in English as a tool for social mobility through better employment and economic opportunities than Spanish. This understanding nurtured the position of English as a High language. The 1930s also witnessed the beginning of a series of immigration waves to the United States in search of better living conditions. Since knowing English improved the chances of succeeding in cities like New York and Chicago, English language skills retained a prestige on a plane in which Spanish could not compete. Even President Roosevelt stressed the immigration issue in the letter addressed to Gallardo in 1937:

> Puerto Rico is a densely populated Island. Many of its sons and daughters will desire to seek economic opportunity on the mainland or perhaps in other countries of this hemisphere. They will be greatly handicapped if they have not mastered English (in Osuna, 1945:376).

The 1930s also witnessed an increase in political repression against those opposed to the American sovereignty over Puerto Rico (Bosques-Perez, 2003). Many members of the pro-independence movement, particularly the *Partido Nacionalista* were jailed and killed. The movement was criminalized by Puerto Rican and American authorities; their stances on the English question dismissed as extreme. Thus, in spite of the enhanced educational role for Spanish, the diglossic relationship between Spanish and English did not disappear with the reforms and continued to be linked to the colonial relations.

Educational Language Gap, 1949–1968

The relationship between English educational and social uses was reversed in 1949. Since then until today, the value for ELAG has been negative, reflecting a larger social than educational role. Villaronga's policy reduced the educational value of English to that of a tertiary language, while the social use had increased to that of a secondary language with primary elements. The value for ELAG was -0.43, which reflected the educational underuse of English. ELAG reached its lowest point in 1965 (-0.55) when the social use of English increased while the educational use remained untouched.

Table 5.1 English Educational Policies in Puerto Rico

Year	Policy	English Social Use	English Educational Use	ELAG
1900	Brumbaugh	0.12 tertiary/secondary	0.44 secondary	0.32 overuse
1904	Falkner	0.20 tertiary/secondary	0.89 primary	0.69 overuse
1908	Dexter	0.20 tertiary/secondary	1.00 primary	0.80 overuse
1916	Miller/Huyke	0.31 secondary	0.67 secondary/primary	0.36 overuse
1934	Padín	0.53 secondary	0.44 secondary	0.09 flat
1949	Villaronga	0.53 secondary/primary	0.10 tertiary	-0.43 underuse
1965	Villaronga	0.65 secondary/primary	0.10 tertiary	-0.55 underuse
1969	Mellado	0.65 secondary/primary	0.22 tertiary/secondary	-0.43 underuse
1991	Aponte	0.57 secondary/primary	0.22 tertiary/secondary	-0.35 underuse
1996	Fajardo	0.65 secondary/primary	0.32 secondary	-0.33 underuse
2001	Rey	0.65 secondary/primary	0.22 tertiary/secondary	-0.43 underuse

The relatively small role for English in Puerto Rico's public schools helped the PPD secure the loyalty of pro-independence sectors that valued the defense of the Puerto Rican culture. For instance, the PPD created the Institute for Puerto Rican Culture (as opposed to the Puerto Rican Institute of Culture) and gave its direction to Ricardo Alegría, a self-professed *independentista*, although not a member of the Puerto Rican Independence Party. At the same time, the PPD strengthened the political persecution against the pro-independence parties, which helped bring about the electoral collapse of the movement during the 1960s. The other political opposition, loyal to U.S. interests, emerged.

Educational Language Gap, 1969–Present

The year of 1969 marked the beginning of a new paradigm in educational language policies in Puerto Rico. The new policy reasserted the role of English in public education and reintroduced it as a medium of instruction, albeit in a limited capacity. ELAG reflected the change experiencing a reduction in value to -0.43, which represented a closer relationship between the social and educational values of English. ELAG experienced another brief reduction in 1991 to -0.35 when the social use of English decreased, due to its elimination as an official language by Governor Hernández Colón. It soon returned to its previous value when Rosselló reinstated English as an official language in 1993, increasing again the value for social use. This event would have increased the value of ELAG by enlarging the social use, and consequently, the distance between the social and educational values of English. However, the Bilingual Citizen Project, a neo-Americanization policy, increased the value for educational use, neutralizing the increase in social use. The new value for ELAG became -0.32.

The end of the Bilingual Citizen Project in 2001 reduced again the educational use of English and produced an increase in ELAG to -0.43, which meant a return to its 1995 value.

In sum, the value of ELAG for the period between 1969 and 2013 remained constant most of the time at -0.43.

6

Language Stakeholders

We now turn our attention to the influence of language stakeholders over educational policies in Puerto Rico. The institutional characteristics of the education department affected their chances of influencing the actions of policymakers. The three fundamental aspects of those characteristics were the autonomy of the education secretary, the centralization of the school system, and the participation of teachers in educational policy. Sometimes variations in those factors resulted in policy changes that showed relative shifts of influence among the language stakeholders.

The Americanization Policy, 1898–1948

Puerto Rico had over two hundred urban and rural schools around the island when the Spanish-Cuban-American War exploded. The system fit the profile of a rural country at the turn of the nineteenth century. It was highly decentralized with virtually no central educational authority. Schools varied sharply and many depended solely on one teacher. The occupation of American troops during the summer of 1898 provoked the closing of many schools, the departure of many teachers to Spain, the dissolution of government educational offices, and the closing down of higher education institutions. Because there was a shortage of schools and teachers, most Puerto Rican children were not enrolled in schools by the beginning of the twentieth century.

Administrators and the Americanization Policy

The American military government that ruled Puerto Rico until 1900 approved the school laws of 1899 in order to rebuild and centralize the public school system. The school laws created the Insular Board of Education, a central agency directed by a board president, named by the military governor. The laws also created and delegated much power to local school boards, one for each of Puerto Rico's 77 municipalities. School boards were composed of elected trustees who served two-year terms. The trustees were encouraged to establish public schools, and received the authority to hire teachers but also the responsibility to pay them. The president of the insular board of education could also appoint teachers. Nevertheless, this system failed to create the expected number of public schools and to hire enough teachers. Poor economic conditions, aggravated by hurricane San Ciriaco in 1899, prevented school districts and local boards from assigning resources for school buildings, teachers' salaries, and textbooks. It is likely that the failure to create schools was also influenced by opposition from most boards to the imposition of the English language and the failure of the school laws to adapt to Puerto Rican conditions (Osuna, 1949:131). For instance, the winter academic break ended in the first week of January. This meant that teachers and students had to attend classes on one of the biggest Puerto Rican Holidays of the year, the Three Kings Day (January 6th).

The failure of the school boards system, coupled with the growing influence of the education commissioner under the Foraker Act of 1900, paved the way for the development of a highly centralized school system in Puerto Rico. It consisted of three levels: central (commissioner of education), middle (supervisors and superintendents), and local (school boards, municipal commissioners and school principals).

The Organic Act of 1900 (Foraker Act) replaced the insular board of education with the department of education, headed by an education commissioner. It did not detail the commissioner's duties, so successive legislation gave him specific and ample powers over the educational system. The school laws of 1901 centralized the administration of schools even further, gave the commissioner ample powers over the system, and subordinated the local school boards to central office jurisdiction. The commissioner's duties, contained under section 23 of the 1901 School Laws, included the appointment of supervisors and superintendents, the preparation and promulgation of all courses of study, the administration of all examinations, the issuing of teaching licenses, the selection and purchasing of all textbooks, and the approval of plans for all school buildings (Osuna, 1949:140).

The commissioners of education between 1899 and 1948 held a great deal of autonomy from the governors. The U.S.president nominated the person for the post and the U.S. senate confirmed him, just like any other presidential nomination. Hence, once a person went through the process and the president spent political capital to support him, a commissioner of education in Puerto Rico held his post with much authority and security. Also, commissioners came with a colossal mission that, had it not failed, may have changed the history of Puerto Rico and the U.S. itself. The undertaking was no other than to transform Puerto Rican society and culture by the assimilation of an Anglo-Saxon cosmology. The practical objective for many in Washington was for Puerto Rico to become a state of the union. Governors of Puerto Rico realized that in educational policymaking, commissioners held practically a free reign. Education commissioners held their posts for an average of 3 years and 10 months between 1899 and 1948 while governors held theirs for 2 years and 7 months. Governors held their posts for less time than education commissioners, probably because there were fewer incentives to keep the post, or because it was easier to remove them. In fact, governors had little control over the determination of educational language policies. Education commissioners had the power to determine and enforce drastic changes without any other authority than their own and the trust of the U.S. president. Hence, when education commissioners revised the educational language policies in 1904, 1907, 1916, and 1932, nobody could stop them (see Table 6.1). Some commissioners' circular letters became executive decrees with the strength of laws, bypassing all other forms of decisionmaking institutions in Puerto Rico.

Education commissioners were interested in the efficient development of a new school system based on the organization of American schools, the improvement of literacy, and the modification of the children's cultural habits through a new language and a new national identity.

The daunting task of developing a new school system became the principal challenge but also the main achievement of education commissioners. Commissioners' annual reports, circular letters, and press releases consistently emphasized the growth in numbers of schools, teachers, and pupils on the island. In 1898 Puerto Rico had 525 public schools, 765 teachers, and 29,172 children in attendance. By 1914, there were 4,336 public schools, 2,564 teachers, and 207,010 children attending schools (Bainter, 1914:372). This eightfold increase in schools was directed by a central office staff of only ten people: a commissioner, an assistant commissioner, a disbursing officer, a secretary, two stenographers, a bookkeeper, a shipping clerk, a messenger, and a janitor (Osuna, 1949:137). In 2010, the department had over 30,000 administrative posts, 40,000 teachers, 1,540 schools, and 485,000 students.

Table 6.1 Pivotal Circular Letters

Topic	Commissioner	Year
English became the medium of instruction for all grades	Roland Falkner	1904
English became the medium of instruction from 5th grade	Paul Miller	1916
Spanish became the medium of instruction in grammar school	José Padín	1934
Spanish became the medium of instruction for all grades	Mariano Villaronga	1949

Commissioners were not interested in establishing just any kind of system; they intended it to be a reproduction of the American school structure. They managed to establish coed classrooms, a graded system, and free schooling. However, American administrators encountered several obstacles, similar to those faced at the time in tUnitehe Philippines (Barrows, 1907). The school day in many areas could only extend to a half day for lack of buildings and teachers, compulsory attendance could not always be enforced, since many children were required to work by their poor families, and teachers resented the changes in academic schedules, particularly the ten-month and later nine-month year, which kept them without pay for two or three months a year.

The hardest policy to enforce was the imposition of American cultural values and habits. Two aspects were salient in this process: patriotism and language. Most writings of the time indicated that the school system was partially successful in developing a sense of connection with American nationalistic symbols and historical figures. Children were required to salute the U.S. flag, learn the Star Spangled Banner, recite the Pledge of Alliance, and study about U.S. presidents as if they were part of their shared history. The language dimension of the Americanization policy aroused a greater public controversy. While there were public outcries against instilling American patriotism, they paled compared to the language issue. Language became a symbol of the colonial relation between Puerto Rico and the United States. The matter polarized Puerto Rican society: the pro-statehood groups favored the instructional use of English; the independence movement rejected it; the autonomist sectors generally rejected it but some supported it.

The supervisors represented the link between the commissioner and the local communities, be them school boards, municipalities or individual schools. Initially there were only English supervisors, hired in 1899 to oversee the progress of English instruction and report back to the commissioner. They were all Anglophones from the U.S. Their duties included: holding teachers' meetings regarding English instruction, distributing teachers' salary checks, administering teachers' license examinations, rendering monthly reports about schools' conditions, representing the central office in enforcing school laws, and receiving feedback petitions and complaints from teachers and community members (Osuna, 1949:144–5). Although they were introduced as the liaison between local and central authorities, supervisors were really the heads of their school districts and their loyalties lay with the central office. Not surprisingly, they met resistance form teachers, who were not accustomed to direct supervision and resented the imposition of a new language and method.

The school laws of 1903 renamed the English supervisor post to schools superintendent, which in turn was changed later to supervising principal. Supervising principals became supervisors again in 1915. New supervising positions were added in 1913, to include Spanish, manual training, domestic science and household economy, and playgrounds and athletics supervisors (Osuna, 1949:147). Supervisors were appointed by the commissioner, generally from the ranks of teachers, and appointments were justified in terms of training and administrative experience (Osuna, 1949:149). There were no formal qualifications for supervisors until 1909, when a principal's license became a requirement by the new laws. Commissioners frequently consulted them about language policy implementations. In a typical letter, Falkner addressed his superintendents:

> We want to extend our English grade work but do not wish to approve any plan which we know will give unsatisfactory results... Immediately upon receipt of this letter kindly let us know just what you plan to do in English in each of your towns next year (Circular Letter 421, 1907).

However, while they were consulted, they had no vote on final decisions. Their role was to represent the commissioner, enforce the department's policies, and report back to the central office. Their work was very important for policy implementation, and whatever success the English policy achieved was in great deal due to the supervisors.

Supervisors and teachers faced some common challenges. For supervisors, knowing English was a prerequisite, and the ratio of American vs. Puerto Rican supervisors was large. In 1912, for instance, 50 percent of all superintendents were born in the United States. The proportion of American superintendents was higher during the early years of Falkner's policy, where only a handful of Puerto Rican teachers had been trained in English. The competition with Americans was much higher for superintendents than for teachers. Supervisors were expected to comply with departmental policies and had little job security. On the uncertain nature of their posts, the school laws of 1901 read:

> Supervisors' duties shall be prescribed by the Commissioner of Education and their services may be dispensed with at any time he may deem it necessary for the good of the schools to do so... (in Osuna, 1949:146).

A large number of departmental circular letters were directed to them with instructions related to the English policy. Falkner asked superintendents for progress reports on their districts' English instruction, statistics on English teachers, and specific information about English teachers' placements within their districts. Those letters and instructions reflect the strong pressure which supervisors faced to follow the educational language policy established by education commissioners from the central office.

The first school laws, approved in 1899, established that each municipality would have a school board, composed of three trustees elected during municipal elections. Their duties included the employment of rural and graded teachers, principals and janitors for their schools, and holding, under their corporate names, land and property for school purposes (Osuna, 1949:150). Supervisors were ex-officio members of the boards, with voice but no vote, and shared with the boards the decisions over assigning teachers to schools. On one level school boards were administrative posts that helped establish the new educational system. On another level, they were elective organisms that represented the communities' interests and were influenced by politics. Teachers' participation in school boards was low, as evidenced by the large turnover of teachers each time a new party controlled the municipal elections. Politicians, not teachers, controlled the school boards. Hence, the decentralized nature of school boards did not preclude the exclusion of teachers at local levels.

School board members' interests differed throughout the island, but being elected posts their preferences tended to reflect their political affiliations. The *Partido Unión* controlled most of the island's municipalities and school boards from 1904 to 1924. Since the party was openly against English as instructional medium, most school boards protested Falkner's policy. The fact that education commissioners addressed their circular letters to school boards in Spanish, while supervisors were always addressed in English and teachers mostly in English, shows an admission from commissioners that most school boards resented the use of English.

In the end, local school boards were ineffective in enforcing school policies. They lost a great deal of power with the Foraker Act and especially with the school laws of 1901, by virtue of the many duties assigned to the education commissioner. Their participation in school policy also decreased as the decisionmaking process shifted towards the center. Hence, the new political and educational institutions helped to reduce the school boards' influence over the development and enforcement of educational policy. Their leverage shrunk by eliminating most boards' policymaking duties, by giving supervisors more control over their school districts' daily operations, by increasing the commissioners' areas of influence, and by reducing the accountability of administrators' actions. The reduction of local communities' inherence over educational policies allowed for the rapid intensification of the English language policy after 1904. Local communities lacked effective institutional mechanisms and influential language stakeholders to curb an imposing wave of transculturation, the likes of which had not been seen in Puerto Rico since the early days of the Spanish colonization. Local school boards formally disappeared in 1919 and were replaced by the municipal commissioners of education, whose job security rested entirely on the commissioner's hands. Naturally, they remained loyal to the central office dictates.

Each municipal commissioner, later renamed school director, was appointed by the town mayor with the advice and consent of the municipal assembly. Municipal commissioners represented their municipalities at the school district level, and made recommendations to the education commissioner about the hiring of teachers (Osuna, 1949:280).

By the time Miller assumed the leadership of the department in 1915, Commissioners Falkner, Dexter, and Bainter had obtained legislation to expand the commissioners' roles from their original description in the Foraker Act. Miller's department continued to function as a highly centralized institution with few participation channels for teachers and parents. However, there were some important differences between Falkner's school system of 1900 and Miller's system of 1915. More specifically, by 1915 two educational sectors were increasing their inherence over educational policies: teachers and parents. The education department under Miller remained closed and centralized, but it opened some limited spaces and moved slightly away from centralization relative to the Falkner period.

The emergence of Miller's policy was affected more by changes in participation than in decentralization. The Jones Act, relative to the Foraker Act, assigned the commissioner more formal powers over policy determination, hiring of teachers, curriculum development, and budget matters (Table 6.2). On formal terms, the new law increased the commissioner's power within the education department. In reality, however, the Jones Act delimited the commissioner's duties, and effectively limited the scope of his actions. There was more room for interpretation of duties under the Foraker Act than under the Jones Act, and education commissioners had used their leverage during the former as executive council members to continually expand their range of influence in the educational system (Negrón de Montilla, 1990).

The area where the Jones Act truly reduced the commissioner's influence was in the elimination of the executive council and, hence, the commissioner's legislative role. It terminated his direct formal inherence on educational affairs of the legislative branch and reduced his overall political clout. Post-Jones Act institutional changes influenced the maintenance of Miller's policy during 18 years and two other commissioners. The fact that Huyke did not overturn Miller's policy is surprising, considering his enthusiastic attention to the learning of English. The amount of circular letters regarding the importance of English and stressing American values is larger than that of any of his predecessors. Huyke insisted on having the children speak English during recess; on the creation of English clubs within and outside the school; on establishing an English test as a high school graduation requirement; on expecting teachers to speak English among themselves; and on holding all departmental written communications, at all levels, in English. However, he did not return the educational language policy to Falkner's approach because the post of education commissioner had lost enough political power in policy formation to language stakeholders such as the *Asociación de Maestros de Puerto Rico* and the *Partido Unión* that reverting Miller's policy would have been too costly.

Table 6.2 Constitutional Duties of Education Commissioners

Year and Law	Title	Constitutional Duties
1900, Foraker Act: Named by U.S. President, Confirmed by U.S. Senate	Commissioner of Education	–in charge of public education –approve all expenses –perform other functions given by law –submit annual reports to Governor and U.S. Congress
1917, Jones Act: Named by U.S. President, Confirmed by U.S. Senate	Commissioner of Education	–lead public education –approve budget –prepare all courses of study, subject to approval by the Governor –prepare bylaws for selection of teachers –approve teachers' appointments by school boards –perform other duties given by law
1947, Law of Elective Governor: Named by P.R. Governor, Confirmed by P.R. Senate	Commissioner of Instruction	–lead public education –approve budget –prepare all courses of study, subject to approval by the Governor –prepare bylaws for selection of teachers –perform other duties given by law
1952, Free Associated State, *ELA*: Named by P.R. Governor Confirmed by P.R. Senate	Secretary of Instruction/ Education	–no mention of duties

The supervisory position changed little during Miller's tenure. Supervisors still represented the link between the education department and local communities, from school boards to municipal offices. Ultimately, supervisors owed their allegiance to the central office. According to Osuna (1949:274), the term "supervisors" is misleading, since their roles were more of inspectors for their employer than leaders of school regions.

While Miller did not modify the nature of the position, he increased the ratio of native to imported supervisors, which improved relations with Puerto Rican teachers. This aspect became important as the AMPR became increasingly involved in educational legislation and educational policymaking.

The office of the commissioner of education experienced no fundamental changes from the Jones Act of 1917 until the 1930s. The education commissioner was still appointed by the U.S. president with the consent of the senate. Education commissioners still implemented the educational public policy through decrees or "circular letters."

Padín made full use of the post's power on 1931 and implemented through circular letters and other means a reformulation of the department that still persists to this day. He divided the department in two areas: technical and administrative (Osuna, 1949:271). He then placed one assistant commissioner at the head of each division. The general effect of the reform was a relative decentralization of the department's operations, by delegating several tasks that were previously concentrated on the commissioner's office. It also increased the participation of larger sectors of the educational system through the creation of jobs in the newly created offices of assistant commissioner. It also injected a dose of professionalism to the department's operations, since it promoted specialization in services and reduced the inherence of administrators over strictly instructional decisions. The Administrative Division included the Bureau of Property and Accounts, the Bureau of Municipal School Affairs, the Bureau of Personnel, and the Division of School Lunch (Circular Letter 2, 1931). The Technical Division contained the Bureau of Supervision, the Bureau of Adult and Extension Services, the Bureau of Research and Statistics, and the Bureau of Personnel (the area shared by both divisions). The commissioner retained extensive powers, so it would be inaccurate to describe the new structure as decentralized. Nevertheless, relative to the previous thirty years of the department's existence, Padín's reform provided a qualitative difference in the way daily operations were held and in the way policies were determined, thus moving the decisionmaking process a notch away from the otherwise nearly absolute centralization.

Besides the 1931 reforms, Padín established a more open system of decisionmaking, which included consultation of teachers (individuals and organized) and Parent-Teacher Associations (PTA's) before implementing major educational changes. The more participatory structure was influenced by his own style but also by the experience of his predecessor's last years in the post, in which the break with the

AMPR obstructed the commissioner's capacity to run the school system's operations efficiently and showed the need to cultivate a working relationship with the teachers' guild. Commissioner Huyke had faced opposition from the AMPR, which had damaged his public image and his capacity to receive cooperation from the teachers. The AMPR had achieved some important goals since 1912 that could not be easily reversed by any commissioner.

Padín also faced pressures from colonial administration and form Washington to pursue a language rationalization policy. If Puerto Rico was to develop stronger political and economic ties with the United States, the continued use of Spanish in the island would have reduced the efficiency of government operations. Thus, the pressures on education commissioners from U.S. presidents and from P.R. governors were to emphasize the use of English. Governors Roosevelt, Gore, and Winship, expressed their dissatisfaction with the emphasis on Spanish. In fact, Padín stated publicly how surprised he was of being reappointed in 1934, right after the announcement of his educational policy. The pressures for language rationalization clashed against the teachers' influence and decentralizing institutional changes, and curbed his drive towards an all-Spanish instruction.

The 1931 reforms, coupled with an opening of participatory channels, established a central office where decisions were made within specialized technical areas with active consultation from teachers and, to a lesser extent, parents. The result was a more participatory decisionmaking apparatus with increased decentralization. The relative increases in openness and decentralization had two important effects on policymaking procedures. First, they allowed for an expansion in policy influence by non-administrative sectors, particularly the teachers, through the AMPR. Since one of the theoretical propositions of this study is that the inclusion of non-administrative educational sectors tends to reduce pressures from state agencies towards language rationalization, we expect that the increased inclusion of teachers in language policymaking would provoke a tendency towards a reduction in ELAG, which in fact occurred. Second, the specialization of duties between administrative and technical areas split the decisionmaking process and separated instructional from administrative matters, which reduced the influence of purely administrative perspectives from educational decisions. Besides, it also shifted part of the decisionmaking process to lower hierarchical levels, since the newly created technical division took over some of the duties previously held at the highest level of the hierarchy.

The reforms also exposed the supervisors to current theories. They helped to professionalize the post and to reduce the resentments between superintendents and teachers. Teachers perceived superintendents as hostile inspectors, loyal to the commissioner and unresponsive to lower-levels of the hierarchy. The reforms included the requirement to take courses in the supervision of instruction at the University of Puerto Rico (Osuna, 1949:276).

The superintendents (the term used for supervisors during Padín's tenure), and their representatives (assistant superintendents), faced strong pressures to respond to central office commands. Education commissioner's circular letters continued to delineate specific instructions to superintendents, to be passed along and enforced at lower levels. Thus, while the supervisory post was improved in terms of technical skills through college courses, stricter requirements, and specialization, the nature of the post within the department's hierarchy changed only slightly and its capacity for independent involvement in policymaking remained low. Superintendents responded more to central educational purposes than to local community or municipal interests, in educational policies in general, and in language approaches in particular.

The post of municipal commissioner was renamed school director with the reforms, but the nature of the officer's duties remained intact. School directors were still appointed by the town mayors with the consent of the municipal assemblies. They represented the links between the central office and the municipal school regions, and their roles concentrated on enforcing directives from the central office, while presenting feedback and advice to the commissioner about local conditions. Like the supervisors, municipal commissioners had minor roles in decisionmaking, so their preferences had little impact in educational policy.

Teachers and the Americanization Policy

The conditions of the teaching profession in Puerto Rico at the turn of the twentieth century included low job security, low pay, reduced classroom autonomy, and no national teachers' union. Those poor working conditions created biases against teacher participation in policy formation by making participation more costly than abstention.

Puerto Rican teachers' gloomy job security expectations were caused by five factors. First, there was no systematic process of merit for hiring and promoting teachers. Some teachers were soldiers that landed with the troops in 1898, who had no other teaching credentials than being native speakers of English. They took the places of many native teachers.

Superintendents recommended the hiring of teachers while the education commissioner determined the final decisions. Evaluations of job performances depended on superintendents' and commissioners' perspectives, which allowed for arbitrary and discriminatory decisions. For instance, Miller made public in 1919 that he would not hire any university graduate who sympathized with the pro-independence ideology, in a clear violation of the right to freedom of speech protected by the Jones Act of 1917 and the U.S. constitution (Negrón de Montilla, 1990:185). He even requested a list of all the college students' names who had petitioned an independence resolution from the Puerto Rican legislature that year, in order to guarantee the students' exclusion from the school system. Second, teaching licenses were granted on temporary bases, so renewals or reappointments could be denied relatively easily. Thus, teachers who did not follow the department's official policies risked not being hired or not having their licenses renewed. Third, the mandatory annual English exam placed a new burden on teachers. Teachers received some incentives to learn the language, such as time off and commendations, but were mostly burdened with the new requirements. They were expected to study the language after school hours, and to receive lessons from American English teachers during the weekends and summer months. Teachers were encouraged to read books in English and submit reviews to their supervisors. Besides the extra work, time dedicated to learning English could not be dedicated to other profiting enterprises, such as summer and weekend jobs, which many teachers needed to compensate for their low salaries.

The expanding school system was in constant need for teachers, particularly those who could teach in English. In 1901 for example, only 22 out of 129 candidates passed the certification exams (Brumbaugh, 1901). The lack of Puerto Rican teachers who could fulfill the language requirements prompted the fourth element that jeopardized their job security: the replacement of Puerto Rican teachers by American teachers. Even Brumbaugh expressed concern about the large number of American teachers relative to Puerto Rican teachers:

> I could not open all the (800 new) schools because I could not find 800 teachers, and I did not want to bring from the United States a larger number of teachers (1901:29).

The importation of teachers increased the competition for the best teaching jobs, in terms of pay and location. Some of the best paying teaching jobs included high schools and special English posts, many of which were occupied by American teachers. High school jobs were not just better paid, but were also located in the urban centers, preferred by most.

Finally, teachers' job security was also threatened by political matters within local school boards. The school boards were the last remnants of a decentralized educational system that included minimal participation from teachers. Thus, decisions regarding teachers' placements (not hiring), which in 1916 remained largely in the hands of school boards, evidenced little influence from rank and file teachers.

This problem was also acknowledged by government administrators, such as Governor Hunt during his third message to the joint session of the legislative chambers in 1904. Hunt argued in favor of more guarantees to teachers, so their destinies would not be so determined by politics (Rigual, 1967:36).

Miller summarized this problem to the supervisors:

> It appears from last year's annual report that... 30.4% of the total number (of teachers) in the service was not returning to the same municipality... The principal reason for such changes is said to be due to political considerations. Wherever there was a change of the party in power there were sweeping changes in the teaching corps. Changes in certain municipalities would have been far more marked had teachers not insured their tenure for the current year by financial contributions to local political committees (Circular Letter 115, 1916).

Teaching salaries were low (Table 6.4) and the lack of a teachers' union precluded wage collective bargaining until after 1912. Puerto Rico suffered at the beginning of the twentieth century high unemployment levels, prevalent illiteracy (around 70 percent), and a struggling economy. U.S. investments in sugar cane rapidly replaced local capitalists, particularly those involved in coffee production. The change from Spanish to American sovereignties in 1898 produced a relocation of export markets for Puerto Rico. The European markets became more expensive while the American market became cheaper. However, the American market was not interested in Puerto Rican coffee, which was the main crop of the island, and whose main market was Southern Europe. The Americans bought their coffee from South America. From Puerto Rico, they wanted sugar (Quintero, 1984). The capitalist economy replaced the plantation economy and with it the island's main socioeconomic relations. Impersonal corporations eliminated the paternalistic haciendas, which kept most of the population in poverty but reproduced established economic roles for most. The new economic relations disintegrated the old informal social insurance systems, such as the quasi-familiar relationship between owners and peasants. Many Puerto Rican investors and landowners were ruined by debt. Thousands of workers lost their jobs and were forced to relocate to the emerging work areas, mostly in the sugar-producing coastal zones (Solís, 1994). The teaching profession reflected those changes in several ways. First, overall economic conditions offered few employment choices, so a low-paying teaching job was better than no job at all. Second, large migrations from the mountainous countryside to the coastal urban centers redefined the school's place within the community. Teachers' status gradually evolved from respected (if meagerly paid) and central members of their communities, into anonymous government employees in large and rapidly changing urban communities.

Classroom autonomy, traditionally large under the Spanish school system, was reduced by the centralized American school system. Osuna describes how difficult it was for teachers to adapt to a centralized system, since before the American system, "every teacher was a rule unto him or herself and did as he or she pleased irrespective of authority" (1949:95). A new level of teacher supervision was added with the establishment of the English supervisor posts (occupied by American teachers). Also, commissioners' circular letters specified how to run language courses, from textbooks to time allotments to daily homework. Circular letters covered every possible topic, even drawings on how to build a latrine. This is not to say that teachers did not have practical leeway within the boundaries of their schools, particularly in remote rural schools that received little supervision. Nevertheless, their autonomy was reduced relative to what they were accustomed.

The Puerto Rican educational system offered strong incentives against teachers' collective action. In 1898 teachers assembled with nonsystem actors at the Tapia Theater in San Juan and discussed their concerns about the continuation and reformation of education in Puerto Rico. The school laws of 1899 provoked a teachers' assembly that asked the governor to validate the teaching licenses obtained under Spanish rule and to receive pay for the two months of summer, among other things. Some of their wishes were granted, but those educators who challenged the school system's main objectives faced strong obstacles (Maldonado, 2001). Teachers struggled to create a union since at least 1900, when a series of articles published in *La Educación Moderna* delineated the attempts to create a Puerto Rican teachers' union (Negrón de Montilla, 1990:74–75). The paper even included a registration form for a national teachers' assembly to be celebrated in a near future. It would not be until July 8, 1911, that the *Asociación de Maestros de Puerto Rico* was created, from the fusion of two teachers' organizations: the *Asociación de Maestros*, founded in 1909 in Mayagüez, and the *Asociación Insular del Magisterio*, founded in 1910 in San Juan (Rodríguez Bou, 1960:399).

The policy effects of the collective organization of teachers were felt more strongly during Miller/Huyke's policy than during Falkner's. In fact, the transition to the former was in great deal caused by legislative pressures of the AMPR. By the year of the AMPR's creation, the Falkner policy had been in effect for six years. Because collective organizations take some time before they mature as institutions and become effective lobbyists, teacher participation was negligible for most of the Falkner policy period, was individual and lacked collective presence.

Among the AMPR's main objectives at its creation were: to produce legislation that would systematize the hiring process; to establish Spanish as the instructional medium; to increase the school year from nine to ten months (and with it the teachers' pay); to increase teachers' salaries; to establish permanent licenses (tenure); to produce legislation in favor of a pension system; to create scholarships for teachers; and to establish a set number of paid absent days (Rodríguez Bou, 1960:400). The AMPR, from its inception until 1946, approved an annual resolution rejecting the use of English as the instructional medium.

The AMPR's original goals reflect two broad concerns: material improvement of the teaching class and change of the educational language policy. Teachers' poor material conditions had discouraged the creation of the association, and had erected barriers against teachers' participation in educational policy.

After its creation, the AMPR exerted influence in educational issues through the lower house, especially during the *Partido Unión's* dominance between 1904 and 1928. The influence was most evident in two bills approved in 1913 and 1915, which addressed the use of English in schools. In 1913 the AMPR pressed for legislation eliminating the annual English exam requisite, and legislation reinstating Spanish as the medium of instruction. The 1915 bill attempted to establish Spanish in schools and in courts. All bills were vetoed by the executive council, but they had a direct impact on the educational policies following the Falkner period. Miller's policy showed the effects of the 1913 and 1915 legislative efforts in reducing the role of English, and even Huyke, a fervent supporter of English in schools, did not reverse the changes.

Table 6.3 P.R. Education Budget, 1900–1923

Year	Budget (million US dollars)	Change	Taxes Collected (million US dollars)	% of Taxes Collected
1900	.377		N/A	
1901	.530	40.1%	2.096	25.31
1902	.754	42%	3.135	24.03
1903	.804	6.7%	3.236	24.84
1904	.874	8.7%	3.230	27.05
1905	.879	0.6%	3.537	24.85
1906	.906	3.1%	3.860	23.47
1907	.919	1.4%	5.055	18.17
1908	1.093	19%	5.014	21.80
1909	1.428	30.6%	4.886	29.22
1910	1.371	-3.9%	5.247	26.14
1911	1.394	1.7%	5.922	23.54
1912	1.519	8.9%	5.574	27.25
1913	1.815	19.5%	5.708	31.80
1914	2.698	48.7%	6.252	43.16
1915	2.070	-23.3%	5.453	37.97
1916	1.840	-11.1%	5.536	33.24
1917	2.107	14.5%	6.646	31.69
1918	2.365	12.3%	7.097	33.33
1919	3.042	28.7%	7.808	38.96
1920	2.957	-2.8%	10.451	28.29
1921	2.899	-1.9%	13.038	22.24
1922	4.689	61.7%	13.355	35.11
1923	4.835	3.1%	11.163	43.31

Sources: Osuna, 1949:620–621; Miller, Annual Report, 1917.

The period before and after the establishment of the Miller/Huyke policy experienced an increase of teacher, student, and parent participation in educational affairs. This rise, coupled with a slight movement away from absolute centralization, allowed language stakeholders that opposed Falkner's policy to influence the establishment and maintenance of a new policy. Thus, the policy emerged from a reordering of power dynamics combined with a relocation of decisionmaking locus.

There were no significant changes in teachers' job security from the Falkner era. If anything, it decreased due to budgetary constraints after academic year 1913–1914, known as "the year of the big budget" (Osuna, 1949:178). After 1914, budgets were reduced due to a contraction in demand for exports during World War I, which reduced the Puerto Rican government's spending capacity. School budgets did not reach the 1914 levels until 1919, and the 1914 dramatic rate of increase was not improved until 1922 (Table 6.3). Reduced budgets meant less teaching positions, reduced salaries, and more competition.

Besides salaries and number of jobs, the school system lacked a uniform classification structure. The American system introduced categories based on letters, E (excellent), G (good), F (fair), and P (poor). Supervisors appraised teachers' jobs according to the scale, but with no consistent evaluation criteria, which allowed for arbitrary evaluations and inconsistent standards among the various school districts, and encouraged a caste system rather than a unified professional group (Osuna, 1949:180). It is no surprise that one of the AMPR's priorities was the creation of consistent and systematic classification guidelines.

The relevance of low job security and salaries for this study lies on the negative impact on teachers' participation. Low job security inhibits teacher participation, since involvement may attract retaliation from administrators. However, measuring from the involvement in the AMPR, teacher participation increased. This increase cannot be understood as a strengthening of individual teachers' power positions relative to administrators. Higher participation can be better understood as a reaction to the perception of increase in real influence from participation (Duke, et al., 1980). Such a perception derived from the willingness of commissioners to court the AMPR from its very beginnings. Whether the courting responded to a cooptation attempt or to a genuine interest in responding to teachers' interest, the union was taken seriously by the central office from its inception, which eased teachers' fears of joining the organization.

In terms of classroom autonomy, commissioners intensified their specific course instructions, especially after the introduction of new texts or methods. The days of teacher individualism under the Spanish rule were long gone, and teachers became accustomed to receiving detailed guidelines from the central office.

One incentive to join the AMPR was the prospect of regaining some indirect control over classroom operations, since the teachers' union could potentially influence teaching methods, textbooks, and curricula. Under most circumstances, teachers' involvement jeopardizes classroom autonomy since it opens spaces for greater scrutiny by peers and administrators over their classroom activities. Hence, the concern over ceding classroom autonomy typically functions as a deterrent for involvement in policymaking. In the Puerto Rican case, however, participation had the potential of increasing autonomy, since most teachers already had little say over their daily work, while the AMPR's involvement gave them a voice in curriculum development at the central level.

The AMPR grew rapidly in membership, organization, and influence. Membership levels in 1911 were 30.5 percent of all licensed teachers in the island, a significant number for a new organization. Membership was high from the start because any individual holding a teaching license was eligible for membership and because the AMPR consolidated elements of the two unions that existed before it. Membership would reach highs of over 90 percent by the 1940s (Osuna, 1949:337). Besides membership, the union became organized quickly through chapters in every municipality, with elected delegates that represented them at the annual convention during the Christmas Holidays. The delegates elected a president, vice president, and several officers for the board of directors. The organization's first president, Francisco Vicenty, was a known academic and editor of the magazine *La Educación Moderna*, and had publicly opposed the preferential use of English since it was established. Under Vicenty's leadership, the AMPR assumed a prominent role in pressing for legislation to reform existing educational practices, through an alliance with the *Partido Unión*.

In general, relations between the AMPR and the commissioner of education were cordial. Miller, together with the AMPR, created *The Puerto Rico School Review*, a monthly journal that informed teachers about new developments in Puerto Rico's public education. The publication was not critical of the department's basic policies. A common practice for the commissioner was to encourage supervisors to allow teachers to participate in the AMPR, and even scheduled a general meeting of supervisors and school principals to coincide with the AMPR's 1919 annual convention, which fostered the creation of effective communication channels between organized teachers and the central office.

Miller's courteous relations with the AMPR also served as a means to influence the organization's goals. Since his main goals were to continue the Americanization process and to increase schooling opportunities to more children, the department moved to influence the AMPR in three directions. First, Miller encouraged the AMPR to join the U.S.-based National Education Association (NEA), which would reduce the possibility of anti-American postures in the teachers' union. Considering that most teachers were from Puerto Rico while most administrators were American, and that one of the major polemic issues in the school system, the language of instruction, was closely linked to U.S.-Puerto Rico relations, an anti-American posture could have surfaced within the AMPR. In fact it appeared, but failed to dominate the organization's public discourse. While affiliation to the NEA provides only a partial explanation for the moderation of anti-U.S. postures, Miller's frequent encouragements to join it reflects his desire to establish strong ties with American institutions. Second, he attempted to influence the AMPR into focusing on theoretical pedagogical issues, rather than on policy affairs. *The Puerto Rico School Review* avoided policy issues, and joint conferences, such as the one in 1919, emphasized teaching methods rather than general curriculum development or evaluations of teachers' job conditions, like salaries or tenure. By focusing on procedural rather than policy issues, teachers' inputs could be directed towards existing policies and away from alternative policy approaches. Finally, the inclusion of teachers' inputs on certain limited areas provided a sense of ownership to the AMPR that curbed adversarial tendencies. The first considerable public crisis between the education department and the AMPR did not occur until 1926 against Huyke.

Cordial relations moderated, but did not preclude, confrontations with the AMPR in two basic areas: working conditions and instructional medium. Concerns of teachers' low salaries and insecure tenure were frequently presented for consideration at the house of delegates, with modest results. On the language question, by 1915 the AMPR had already pursued or supported three legislative bills aimed at establishing Spanish as a dominant language in schools and other areas. Debates on this issue between the AMPR and the department remained confrontational for years to come.

The dynamics between administrators and the teachers' union were complex and experienced different levels of tension according to the issues. While education commissioners supported and tried to influence the AMPR, some issues were confrontational by nature, and placed administrators and teachers on opposite sides. The balance of power of educational policymaking remained tilted heavily towards the central office side, but the inclusion of an organized teachers' pressure group concluded the commissioner's absolute control over school policy.

The evolution of teachers' working conditions during the 1930s was slow and with mixed results. The areas of policy involvement and job security experienced a modest but steady improvement. Wages recuperated from the economic crisis of World War I but declined again during the 1930s depression. The increase in policy involvement resulted from the strengthening of the AMPR's influence over departmental affairs, while the betterment in job security stemmed from legislation and regulations that systematized the hiring and promotion of teachers. Padín's reforms of 1931 established specific evaluation terms and promotion criteria. He also alleviated the confrontation between the AMPR and the department of education, inherited from Huyke's tenure, by opening the process of policy formation to teachers' and parents' organizations. Salaries began to recover gradually again after 1935.

In the 1930s, Puerto Rican teachers saw an improvement in their job security, a decrease in salaries, and some improvement in their classroom autonomy. The first was due to the approval of new selection regulations in 1932, the second was produced by the contraction in the island's economy, and the third was produced by improvements in the training of supervisors.

The Teacher Selection Bylaws of 1932, presented in circular letter 83, established 10 specific criteria for the nomination of teachers to posts in the educational system. School principals received job applications and selected teachers for their schools, with approval of the education commissioner. The final decision still rested on the commissioner's hands, but the specification of hiring and renewal criteria decreased the principals' capacity to select teachers on arbitrary bases. Moreover, the new bylaws established the teachers' right to appeal before the commissioner. Thus, with all its limitations, the new system improved the teachers' job security by establishing objective hiring criteria based on merit and seniority.

Teachers' wages experienced a decline in 1935, as part of a total reduction in the department's budget. This decade marked the beginning of U.S. aid to education in Puerto Rico, partly because of the detrimental budgetary effect of a shrinking economy, and as part of President Roosevelt's involvement of the federal government in educational programs in the U.S. and its territories. Table 6.4 shows the little progress in teachers' salaries in three decades in Puerto Rico's school system. Low teaching salaries fueled the exodus of teachers to other, better remunerated professions. The popular expression that someone may be "as poor as a rural school teacher" captures the meager living conditions of most teachers during this period. A gradual recovery from the economic depression increased the education department's budget for teachers' salaries after 1936.

Table 6.4 P.R. Teachers' Monthly Salaries (U.S. Dollars)

Title	1907	1915	1935
Principal	80 – 95	75	100
Teachers of English	40 – 60	75	100
Graded Teachers	52 – 70	75	82.25
Rural Teachers	33 – 48	38	67.50

Sources: Puerto Rico Department of Education:Circular Letter 11, 1907; Circular Letter 82, 1915;Circular Letter 2, 1935.

The attempt to change the supervisory emphasis from inspection to support provided a small increase in teachers' autonomy. Superintendents received specialized training intended to improve their relations with teachers. The nature of the supervisory post never fully shifted from inspection to support, but the reform increased the superintendents' receptiveness to teachers' demands and increased the teachers' maneuvering room within their classrooms. Increased classroom autonomy reduces the costs of teacher participation in school policy. Thus, while the increase in autonomy was small, it added an incentive towards the already growing teacher involvement.

The AMPR experienced an increase in its policymaking influence in the years before the introduction of Padín's policy. On the one hand, the AMPR established its presence as a major language stakeholder on its own ground, regardless of the alliance with a political party. On the other hand, the dissolution of the *Partido Unión*'s dominance of legislative affairs shifted the AMPR's area of influence form educational legislation to internal decisionmaking.

The important role of the AMPR in educational affairs became most evident in the crisis with Huyke in 1926. Since the notorious legislative debate of 1915 regarding the bill regulating the use of Spanish and English in Puerto Rico, Huyke had placed himself in opposite sides of the AMPR and of other language stakeholders who favored a greater role for Spanish as instructional medium. His appointment as education commissioner was not welcomed by the AMPR, and their relations from the outset were conflictive. Tensions peaked at the 1926 AMPR's annual convention, where several speakers expressed strong views against the language policy and against Huyke himself. The speakers at the assembly included Gerardo Sellés, president of the AMPR, and Antonio R. Barceló, president of the *Partido Unión*. Barceló described the emphasis on Americanization as shameful and expressed that "our schools, our regional symbols have been forgotten in favor of a false Americanism" (Morris, 1995:36; Negrón de Montilla, 1990:238). Huyke answered in kind and advised supervisors and principals to refrain from taking any active participation in the AMPR's affairs through circular letter 75 of 1927. The impasse, resolved through the intercession of the Insular League of Parent-Teachers Associations, demonstrated the important presence of the AMPR in the operations of the education department.

The emergence of a new political force in 1924, *La Alianza*, reduced the inherence of the AMPR in educational decisionmaking. *La Alianza* merged the *Partido Unión* with a fraction of the *Partido Republicano*. The pact with the *Republicanos* effectively terminated the partnership between the *Unionistas* and the AMPR. Hence, the AMPR's influence on educational policies through legislation decreased after 1924. However, the AMPR's decline in legislative influence was offset by an increased involvement in decisionmaking within the education department itself. The 1926 crisis with Huyke had shown the AMPR's capacity to face the commissioner on strong terms. With Padín's appointment, it gained new ground by being included in a series of surveys and consultations that led to the new policy of 1934.

The AMPR's posture towards the language question remained constant since its creation in 1911: Spanish should be the medium of instruction for all grades in public schools. Padín's policy fell short of that goal, but represented a step closer than the earlier policy and was welcomed by the AMPR. Ironically, it placed the role of English in a similar position to that of Brumbaugh's policy in 1900, which had been criticized by many prominent educators in Puerto Rico.

The fact that someone like Padín, committed to an all-Spanish instruction and backed by the AMPR, did not place Spanish as a primary language in education, testifies to the strong pressures stemming from the central and federal governments towards a language rationalization based on English. The AMPR increased its influence on educational policies but only on a limited basis. Also, the centralized educational system (even with the reforms) placed most decisions ultimately in the hands of the commissioner, who responded to a colonial administration whose goals still included a uniform use of English in Puerto Rican society for its assimilation into the American political system.

Nonsystem Actors and the Americanization Policy

The language question became an essential aspect of the public debate in Puerto Rico about its political status with the United States. Hence, political parties, all of which defined themselves partially or totally by their posture relative to the status issue, intervened constantly to influence the educational language policy in Puerto Rico. Entire political parties became language stakeholders, along with their leaders. Many times they were unsuccessful at influencing policy, but sometimes they managed to partially block initiatives and even impose some of their own. The American colonial administrators held a tight grip over public policy, through their control of the executive and judiciary branches. Puerto Rican politicians controlled partially and, since 1917 totally, the legislative branch. However, there was a centralization of decisionmaking power around the executive branch in the figure of the governor. Governors pursued educational language policies of their own. The result was a highly politicized process in which Puerto Rico's most important political sectors participated actively as language stakeholders.

The strongest supporters of the Americanization policy were the American colonial administrators. Governors assumed their posts with specific instructions from Washington to pursue a policy of cultural assimilation that could pave the way for Puerto Rico's political integration as a state of the union. Governors Guy Henry (1898–1899) and George Davis (1899–1900) promoted the approval of the school laws of 1899, which established, among other things, English as a medium of instruction and required the recruitment of English teachers. Governor Beekman Winthrop (1904–1907) supported Falkner's Americanization school policy of 1905. Winthrop managed to contain the negative reaction by forging an informal alliance with the *Partido Unión* based mostly on promises of greater self-government for the island. Governor Regis Post (1907–1909) supported Edwin Dexter's even wider use of English as an educational medium. Governor Post however, could not sustain the alliance with the *Unionistas*, so he faced strong legislative opposition. Arthur Yager (1913–1921), with the largest tenure of any governor during the Americanization period, held his post during some of the most transcendental moments in Puerto Rico's history. His tenure coincided with U.S. entry into World War I, the granting of American citizenship to Puerto Ricans, and the acquisition of the Virgin Islands from Denmark. His behavior as a language stakeholder reflects an increased sensibility towards the obstacles faced by the imposition of the English language. Yager recommended Miller and supported his educational language policy of reducing the educational use of English in 1916. Governor Reily (1921–1923) recommended Huyke. His tenure disappointed many who expected a shift away from the Americanization policy. Reily became a staunch supporter of the existing educational language policy, persecuted the dissidents, and suppressed separatists.

The turning point of the Americanization policy took place during Governor Theodore Roosevelt, Jr.'s tenure (1929–1932). He supported Padín's nomination as education commissioner in spite of his public views against the Americanization educational policy. Roosevelt approved of Padín's approach as a recognition by American colonial authorities that the cultural assimilation strategy had failed to transform Puerto Rican society to the extent they believed was necessary for full political integration. It also reflected the failure of similar assimilationist programs in the U.S. mainland. Governor Rexford Tugwell (1941–1946), who had been one of the creators of Roosevelt's New Deal, forged a political alliance with the *Partido Popular Democrático,* that controlled the legislature during the 1940s, and his leader Muñoz Marín. Through this alliance the government of Puerto Rico increased its role in the economy by buying or creating several public industries. Tugwell also supported Munoz Marín's cultural nationalist project and anti-separatist policy. Hence, Tugwell agreed with Muñoz Marín's recommendation of Villaronga as commissioner of education in 1946. Tugwell knew that Villaronga would attempt to discontinue the Americanization educational language policy but supported him anyway. This shows the shift in the colonial politics of the United States towards less assimilation and more self-government. At the time, the United Nations Organization pressured colonial powers to recognize their possessions' right for self-determination and linguistic protection. The U.S. congress was considering the bill that allowed Puerto Ricans to elect their governor and the bill that would allow Puerto Rico to approve a constitution. It was only a matter of time for the Americanization policy to come to an end with the consent of the colonial authorities.

The pro-statehood *Partido Republicano* always defended the Americanization policy. They became the strongest supporter of the policy among the political elite and represented a large minority of people who believed that Americanization was synonymous with progress. The party's founder and leader until his death in 1921, José Celso Barbosa used his leverage to promote the assimilation policy and the granting of the American citizenship in 1917. He believed that citizenship would mean that Puerto Rico would become an "incorporated" territory and that statehood would be the logical consequence of it. Neither congress nor the supreme court would interpret it that way, but he never saw the conclusion because of his death. The influence over policy of *Republicanos*, as language stakeholders, was not great. The political institutions offered little space for them to affect language policy. At the level of the Puerto Rican legislature, *Republicanos* played a major role between 1900 and 1904, when they controlled the house of delegates due to the opposition's electoral boycott. They supported the Falkner policy of 1904 and gave their consent to various school laws stemming from it. Governors Charles Allen (1900–1901) and William Hunt (1901–1904) placed prominent *Republicanos* in their cabinets and allowed them to exert some influence over educational language policies. The political institutions provided the space for *Republicanos* to translate some of their preferences over language use into public policy. Their influence was, however, not a necessary factor in producing the Americanization policy, although it provided much needed legitimacy. Their influence diminished significantly from 1902 to 1932, since the *Partido Unión* dominated the house of delegates, renamed house of representatives in 1917, and the senate, created in 1917. Most legislative bills that referred to the language issue during that time rejected the Americanization policy, in spite of the objections from *Republicanos*. They returned as the legislative majority in both houses between 1932 and 1940 by forging an alliance with the *Partido Socialista Obrero*, also pro-statehood. However, their control over the legislative institutions was not enough to translate their language preferences into policy, since by then Padín had relegated the use of English as a medium of instruction to high school only. Their influence came too late, since there was no turning back on a policy that had failed to fulfill its expectations.

The *Partido Unión* dominated the legislative process from 1904 to 1924. Their official preference over language policy was a rejection of the Americanization model, although there were important dissidents like Huyke. *Unionista* leaders like Luis Muñoz Rivera and De Diego became language stakeholders on their own. They presented several bills adopting Spanish as the medium of instruction, although no governor signed them into law. De Diego, who presided over the house of delegates, even founded a private school that used only Spanish as a medium of instruction, in open defiance of the Americanization policy.

The Distribution of Power during the Americanization Period

Policy formation rested almost entirely in the hands of the education commissioner, with no institutional channels for teacher involvement. The Foraker Act and the subsequent school laws placed most policy decisions in the hands of the commissioners, who communicated their decisions through departmental circular letters, as *faits accomplis*. The history of educational policy changes in Puerto Rico is contained in the large number of circular letters written by education commissioners, a practice initiated by Brumbaugh in 1900 and continued uninterruptedly to our days.

The institution of the education department also served a political role. On one hand, commissioners had much autonomy from the governors. On the other hand, they had instructions from Washington about the fundamental objectives of the public school system, and they followed them. The centralized, political, and non-participatory nature of the department of education provoked educational language policies that only a minority supported in Puerto Rico. The political nature of the school system's institutions allowed the U.S government to impose its preferences, particularly those of the war department, which had jurisdiction over Puerto Rico until 1934.

Under these conditions it is not surprising that teachers' interests were all but excluded from school policies. Many of the conditions discussed by scholars of educational administration which discourage teachers from participating were present in Puerto Rico: increased time demands, loss of classroom autonomy, and threats to career advancement (Duke, et al., 1980).

This picture describes a bleak situation for the teaching profession with no representation, job security, or collective bargaining power. But it would misrepresent their condition in Puerto Rican society if we did not consider alternative forums for teachers' expression. Teachers had venues for voicing their concerns by influencing public opinion through the written media and through political parties. The AMPR became the main exponent of teachers' interests and became relevant in the political landscape.

Politicians, pressure groups, and other nonsystem actors, besides the U.S. government, had relatively little influence over educational language policies. The Americanization policy survived for fifty years in spite of the opposition by the most powerful Puerto Rican politicians of the time, whose parties and themselves became relevant language stakeholders. On the other hand, those that favored the Americanization policy had little participation on its conceptualization and implementation. However, their support provided legitimacy to the political project of the U.S. towards Puerto Rico.

The Puertoricanization Policy, 1949–1968

Illiteracy remained a chronic problem in 1949, even after the great strides towards eliminating it since the creation of the public educational system in 1899. There were still large numbers of uneducated people and many communities still lacked access to public education. Also, Puerto Rico experienced a population boom after World War II, coupled by a large migration from the countryside to the coastal cities. Many of these domestic immigrants ended up living in slums that sprang across San Juan, Ponce, Mayagüez, and other major cities. The department responded with an aggressive program of building schools, hiring new teachers and improving the attendance of children. The process sped up after the approval of the Constitution in 1952, which included the right and obligation of every child to receive a good and free education. Article 2, Section 5 states:

> Every person has the right to an education which shall be directed to the full development of the human personality and to the strengthening of respect for human rights and fundamental freedoms. There shall be a system of free and wholly nonsectarian public education. Instruction in the elementary and secondary schools shall be free and shall be compulsory in the elementary schools to the extent permitted by the facilities of the state.

Universal public education became a constitutional right for children and an obligation for the government. The laws made parents responsible for their children's attendance. The department's 1956 annual report claimed that 93 percent of Puerto Rican children went to elementary school. This figure is likely to have been inflated since over half of the island's population lived in poverty and had only meager access to public services, including education. Nevertheless, there is no question that there was a substantial boost in the absolute and relative numbers of children attending schools. One consequence was an increase in the demand for teachers. The AMPR's membership also swelled and its capacity to collect dues increased accordingly. It also strengthened its ties with the ruling coalition, which made it one of the largest, strongest, and most influential unions in Puerto Rico. The AMPR created a teachers' hospital (1959), a teachers' retirement home, and a savings and loan cooperative. Teachers also got a pension fund separate from the government general pension fund.

The University of Puerto Rico (UPR), whose creation in 1903 responded to the need for teachers, reacted by increasing the graduates that occupied the new job openings. Moreover, the faculty of education at the UPR became a center for pedagogical research and innovation. Several UPR professors held the top educational post, like Quintero, Torres, Benítez, and Aragunde.

The process also provoked the growth of the department's bureaucracy. This bureaucracy served the expanding needs of the system, with ever more people working at the central office in San Juan. A pattern emerged in which central and regional office jobs also became places to reward political favors. Hence party politics tainted many administrative decisions. This increased the influence of language stakeholders from the PPD over educational language policies. For instance, the department reacted to the large migration of Puerto Ricans to the United States, particularly New York and Chicago. It established programs for English courses on Saturdays and evenings directed at potential adult migrants. In this way it supported the government policy of encouraging the migration in order to reduce the chronic unemployment in Puerto Rico. The English educational use became part of a larger government policy implemented by the ruling party.

Administrators and the Puertoricanization Policy

Education commissioners became independent from presidential control in 1949, when the first elected governor of Puerto Rico, Muñoz Marín, was sworn in and became the nominating authority. The U.S. president and senate would no longer have a say in either the nomination or the confirmation processes. However, whatever autonomy the education commissioners gained from the president, they lost it to the governor. The commissioner, renamed secretary of public instruction in the 1952 constitution, now required the trust of the governor. Educational policies, particularly about language, became immediately a component of a larger set of public policies determined at *La Fortaleza*, the governor's mansion. That generation of policymakers placed socioeconomic development above everything else. They also viewed education as a fundamental tool for its achievement. Hence, Villaronga gathered a great deal of political power within the ruling party. In addition to that, his department became the center of the PPD's policy of cultural nationalism, the government's second priority. English and Spanish had battled intensely, but now Spanish won decisively. Spanish would no longer be under attack; English sometimes would. The PPD celebrated the island's identity, and being Puerto Rican meant, among other things, speaking Spanish. The educational system remained the fundamental component of the language policy, which now reflected the interests of the Puerto Rican ruling party rather than those of American administrators.

The increased influence by the governor in school affairs, added to Villaronga's tight grip, produced a shift in paradigm in educational language policies. The new educational policy of Puertoricanization resulted from the cultural nationalism of the *Partido Popular Democrático* and Muñoz Marín (Rivera, 2007). From then on, as Lopez Yustos (1997:180) contends, the secretary's decisions became part of the ruling party's electoral platform. In fact, the educational system became one of the pillars that sustained the PPD's political hegemony for 20 years.

The new department did not lose the centralized nature of its decisionmaking processes. The secretary still ruled through circular letters that had the power of laws, like circular letter 10, which established Spanish as the medium of instruction and transformed the educational use for several generations without going through any public scrutiny before its implementation.

Spanish became the medium of instruction, History and Social Studies books were rewritten, and budgets for English teaching were reduced. It celebrated patriotic symbols, people and holidays, as defined by the PPD's cultural nationalism. Villaronga reduced the use of English at the school levels, but also at the central level. He wrote all his circular letters in Spanish, including those dealing only with English. The department virtually ceased to translate its documents into English. This was part of the central government's tendency to replace Spanish in any areas where English had been used. Although the Official Languages Act of 1902 was still in effect and English remained one of two official languages in Puerto Rico, English was rarely used for official purposes.

Villaronga's policy also reflected the central government's preference for efficiency and stability. The policy of a single language would increase efficiency by reducing the costs associated with translating documents, printing materials, and hiring personnel. It would induce stability by producing a consensus policy that could replace the unpopular and controversial Americanization policy. This is true even if it also would produce short-term disruptions during the period of rapid transition, something administrators tend to avoid. However, the transition only produced momentary costs while the new language policy yielded long-term benefits.

The department also transformed the role of supervisors. Villaronga eliminated the post of English supervisor and replaced most Anglophone supervisors and administrators with Spanish speakers. This pattern took place among most government agencies. The newly hired supervisors and administrators became some of the strongest supporters of the Puertoricanization project and the new educational language policy. They did so for several reasons. First, most supervisors saw their positions as representatives of the central office. Hence the majority supported the official educational language policy of Puertoricanization. Second, most newly hired administrators were *Populares*, or partisans of the PPD. Hence, they sympathized with the cultural nationalism and the educational language policy that favored Spanish over English.

Supervisors and other administrators became, once again, indispensable for the implementation of an educational language policy. Meanwhile, English supervisors either lost their jobs or took other posts, such as general supervisors or school inspectors. The department reduced its budget and support towards the teaching of English. Hence, the post of supervisor experienced a 180 degree turn, from having emerged as only English supervisors in 1899, to becoming anything but English supervisors in 1950. It remained, however a position that was highly responsive to the interest of the central office. Supervisory jobs now included several middle level administrative posts, such as directors of educational regions, superintendents, auxiliary superintendents, federal funds supervisors, and program directors.

Sánchez Hidalgo replaced Villaronga as secretary of instruction and continued with the Puertoricanization language policy. The department also continued with the public policy of teaching English for adults who were to migrate to the United States. His actions showed little autonomy from the ruling party's project of encouraging migration to reduce unemployment. He wrote to superintendents:

> During the school year 1959–60 the Department of Instruction will keep in place the teacher exchange program between Puerto Rico and the United States, as authorized by Law Number 37 of May 16 1955. As you remember, the purpose of this law is to help the Puerto Rican migrants to the United States adapt more easily to the linguistic, customs, economic, social and cultural differences (Circular Letter 36, 1959).

Oliveras inserted a measure of decentralization in 1962 by dividing the island into three educational regions: West, Center-West, and South. They eventually became ten regions and included San Juan. Directors of educational regions had little say in fundamental decisions, but they administered large sections of the school system and enjoyed much leverage over the daily administrative decisions. Thus, after the decentralization measures a significant portion of educational decisions were taken at regional levels. This decentralization, however, was not accompanied by increases in participation from teachers at regional or local levels. The relative influence of teachers over educational language policy remained mostly at the central level, through the teachers' union.

Oliveras also placed a great deal of emphasis on English courses for migrant adults, adding television courses. He stated the program's goals as follows:

> The teaching of English for adults pursues the following objectives:
>
> 1. To provide the people who go to the United States to work some knowledge about the English language that may help them manage themselves better during their stay in the Continent.
>
> 2. To try to prepare the immigrants so that they can adapt efficiently to the lifestyle of the American community, giving them for that purpose, orientation about the habits and traditions of the United States (Memorandum 36, 1960).

Secretary Angel Quintero (1965–1968) was a respected scholar who enjoyed a favorable public opinion and received the support of most educational sectors. Governor Roberto Sánchez Vilella did not interfere when Quintero implemented experimental methods such as schools without school years and individualized teaching. He developed some degrees of autonomy from the governor, but it was not institutionalized and depended on Sánchez Vilella's management style.

The PPD's political project gradually lost ground to the pro-statehood movement, which benefited from the break of the populist consensus during the 1960s. Once in power for the first time in 1968 and subsequently, pro-statehood governors pursued educational language policies with rhetoric similar to that of the Americanization period, but with more moderate changes.

Education commissioners held their posts for an average of 6 years and 8 months between 1949 and 1968 while governors held theirs for 10 years. Both increased their average years in office, but the trend clearly reversed from the previous policy period. Now governors stayed longer than commissioners.

Teachers and the Puertoricanization Policy

The teachers' union increased its participation in the department's affairs through the informal alliance with the ruling coalition. The AMPR provided enough incentives to overcome the tendency towards not participation from rank and file teachers. The knowledge that their union had some level of influence over policy decisions increased the union's numbers and the activity of their members. In fact, the AMPR became one of the columns of the populist corporatism that governed Puerto Rico from 1948 to 1968 and an advocate for the cultural nationalist project pursued by the Muñoz Marín administration. Many teachers performed political duties during election times, such as organizing communities, running for office, registering voters, and counting votes. The ruling party intensified the decades-old tradition of using the teachers' societal prestige to promote a political agenda. The Puerto Rican legislature even approved a law allowing teachers who participated as political candidates to receive a paid leave of absence during the election semester. This partial reliance on teachers during electoral campaigns produced a highly politicized system of hiring teachers. Villaronga spoke regularly at the AMPR's annual meetings, showing the close ties between them. The teachers, through their union, supported the educational language policy of Puertoricanization. The support can be understood from two sources. First, their interests were represented at a central level rather than at local boards, which provides incentives for language rationalization. Hence, most teachers, like the AMPR, preferred the use of one language, Spanish, as a medium of instruction. Second, the increased use of Spanish improved the chances of obtaining and maintaining the teaching job for many potential and actual teachers. This is true because by the 1950s still the majority of teachers were monolingual or partially bilingual, so teaching in English meant for them either exclusion or adaptation costs. Also, the discrepancy in salaries between English teachers and the rest was removed, so there were even less incentives to support a significant role for English as a medium of instruction.

Nonsystem Actors and the Puertoricanization Policy

The loss of autonomy by the commissioner and later the secretary meant that nonsystem actors had a greater influence over educational policies than before. The English question was temporarily resolved due to the overwhelming dominance of those groups that favored the use of Spanish as the medium of instruction. The two main political forces in 1952, the autonomists and the separatists, supported the Puertoricanization language policy. They differed over the political relationship with the United States, but agreed that, whether as a territory or as a republic, Spanish was an essential and defining component of the Puerto Rican identity. Hence, the hegemonic PPD implemented Villaronga's educational language policy with no obstacles. The party controlled the governorship, the senate, the house of representatives, the supreme court, most municipalities, the bureaucracy, and the UPR. The PPD, through its leader Muñoz Marín, preferred a uniform single language policy across all schools that supported their cultural nationalist project. Muñoz Marín, a bilingual who was raised in the U.S. and fit the profile of a *niuyorican*, nevertheless pursed a policy against the influence of English over daily affairs. His speech at the AMPR's convention in 1953, known popularly as that of "Agapito's Place" exemplified it (Lopez Yustos, 1997:183). In that speech Muñoz Marín spoke against lexical borrowing, referring to a bar in a small rural town that boasted a sing reading "Agapito's Place," instead of "*El Bar de Agapito.*" Muñoz Marín argued that since none of Mr. Agapito's customers were Anglophones it seemed ridiculous to use such a name.

It is interesting that the PPD, which controlled the legislature and executive between 1949 and 1969, deferred the language question to a circular letter from a cabinet member (the secretary of instruction) and did not bother to approve a law establishing Spanish as the language of instruction or giving it sole official status. It is intriguing because only three years earlier the PPD had gone through many lengths to approve a law (Law 51) that made Spanish the medium of instruction, going over the veto of Acting Governor Manuel A. Pérez, only to be vetoed again by President Truman. The ruling PPD did not submit a similar bill when it controlled the governorship, even though it would not need presidential approval. This is surprising since part of its electoral appeal rested on its promotion of cultural nationalist policies which stressed the role of Spanish as a symbol of the Puerto Rican nation and defended its use over English as a medium of instruction. Even more so, the bill would have enjoyed the support of the pro-independence and nationalist sectors, which were at a high point at the moment. The *Partido Independentista Puertorriqueño* (PIP) arrived in second place during the 1952 election, and its legislators would have supported a pro-Spanish bill. Nevertheless, there was no law resolving the language question. Several reasons explain this. First, the PPD leadership did not want to appear anti-American at a time when the PIP was the second largest electoral force, and the *Nacionalistas* were promoting an armed rebellion to call for international attention amid a stern repression against them which included the lynching of a prisoner in a police department. For instance, the days before the 1948 Election Day, Muñoz Marín had several pro-independence leaders incarcerated. Second, the pro-U.S. faction of the PPD, which eventually joined the pro-statehood party, would not have supported a bill that would perpetuate English to a minor role in public education. Third, the PPD was overwhelmed by a general sense of complacency that believed they would rule forever, so a language law appeared unnecessary since no other party would ever control the department of public instruction.

Even after the end of the PPD hegemony, the decay of the pro-independence movement, and the triumph of the pro-statehood party, the educational language use did not become a law. That is, the pro-statehood PNP did not intend to revert the Villaronga policy through a law by reestablishing English as the medium of instruction, which would have been a predictable move. The PNP, when it attempted to change the policy, did it through circular letters. Even to this day, there is no law regulating the medium of instruction in the public school system of Puerto Rico. In fact, laws regulating the use of languages have been historically rare in Puerto Rico, even though there have been two official languages since 1902, except from 1991 to 1993.

Other nonsystem actors became language stakeholders. The *Academia de la Lengua* stressed its support to the Puertoricanization policy, although it often criticized many lexical forms of the Puerto Rican dialect (Torres, 2002). The *Instituto de Cultura Puertorriqueña*, a government agency, and the *Ateneo Puertorriqueño*, a nongovernment organization created in the nineteenth century, also supported the policy. Their support added legitimacy to Villaronga's approach since the people leading those organizations enjoyed much prestige among the Puerto Rican intelligentsia. However, the establishment of the Puertoricanization policy does not imply that their preferences were translated into government actions. Had they been opposed to his decisions it seems unlikely that they would have been able to change them. They were minor partners of the PPD because they had little institutional access to the process of decisionmaking. Nevertheless, their support provided a great deal of legitimacy to the Puertoricanization policy and defended it in many forums.

The Distribution of Power during the Puertoricanization Period

The policy of Puertoricanization was no less political than the previous one. It just had different objectives. Spanish became a fundamental component of the imagined community of Puerto Rico that the PPD reinvented. It also became a powerful tool against statehood, and it surfaced every time the U.S. congress debated a bill regarding Puerto Rico (Barreto, 2001).

The Law of Elective Governor changed the political institutions of Puerto Rico and altered the way the commissioner of education was chosen since 1949. However, the centralization of the department remained intact. The commissioner's decrees through the circular letters continued to become virtual laws. Administrative posts now belonged to sympathizers of the new administration, but their relative power to the central office did not increase. The most important decree during Villaronga's term was circular letter 10 of 1949, which neutralized any potential attempts to reestablish an all-English curriculum.

The constitution that declared Puerto Rico a free associated state or *Estado Libre Asociado* (ELA) in 1952 erased any mention about the duties of the secretary of public instruction. This omission contrasts with the explicit educational objectives in the constitution's bill of rights, by which every child has a right to a public education that develops his personality to the fullest and strengthens the respect for human rights.

The secretary's duties were determined by law, the first one of which was Law 6 of 1952. However, there were no general school laws approved. The two previous organic acts, the Foraker and Jones Acts, had been fairly detailed about the commissioner's role (Table 6.2). The Jones Act had specified six duties. Besides that, the school laws of 1903 detailed even further the reach of his responsibilities. In fact, those laws were not abolished until 1990. Hence, given that there were no constitutional guarantees of the secretary's powers, he grew more dependent on the actions of the politicians that could increase or reduce his leverage on educational affairs.

Teachers assumed a more prominent role in Puerto Rican politics by the adherence of the AMPR to the ruling coalition of the PPD. The inclusion of their union in public affairs reduced the individual risks of teachers' involvement and increased the benefits of participation. The AMPR regained much public respect and official recognition. Also, teachers experienced a reduction in time demands by eliminating the English course requirements. They also saw a relative increase in classroom autonomy after the reduction in the demands of cultural assimilation. Finally, there was a reduction in the threats to their career advancement by the establishment of merit scales (Duke, et al., 1980). Their inclusion in the government coalition paid off with perks like the establishment of a separate pension fund for teachers in 1951 through Law 218.

The last stage of the Puertoricanization period saw the emergence of an alternative teachers' union, the *Federación de Maestros de Puerto Rico*. The *Federación*, associated with the independence movement, broke the AMPR's monopoly on teacher representation and eventually replaced it.

Puerto Rican politicians now became more influential in educational language policies. The commissioner of education, later secretary of instruction became a position of confidence of a governor, who was himself elected through a partisan process. The PPD achieved a control over Puerto Rico's educational affairs that no political movement had ever reached. It is not surprising then, that the PPD left intact the institutional features of the school system, even though they wrote and approved the 1952 constitution, and ruled uncontested from 1948 to 1968. The PPD, as a language stakeholder, benefited from the centralized, political, and non-participatory nature of the educational system, which allowed them to establish the Puertoricanization policy against the will of several influential language stakeholders.

The Bilingualization Policy, 1969–Present

The end of the populist era and the ascendance of the pro-statehood movement in 1968 tilted the balance of power among language stakeholders in Puerto Rico. Those favoring a larger role of English in Puerto Rican society increased their influence over educational language policies. A societal consensus emerged in Puerto Rico as for the relevance and necessity of bilingual education. English was increasingly perceived as a tool for social mobility. Hence, it provoked a renewed push to increase the educational role of English. However, there remained a strong opposition to English immersion education because the language stakeholders committed to the Puertoricanization project had institutionalized their influence and increased their participation inside and outside the department, so it became impossible to return to an Americanization program. Nevertheless, since there was a considerable fraction of the pro-statehood movement that supported bilingual education through immersion schools, the issue over English use in education was not resolved. Part of the problem stems from the particular variants of bilingual education that dominate the public debate in Puerto Rico. In the debate, bilingual education means either transition or immersion. In the first case, bilingual programs helped Anglophone children who came from the U.S. since the early 1970s to adapt to an all-Spanish school system. This type of bilingual education was generally accepted as necessary and did not provoke controversy. The second case was the main tool of Americanization and generated the biggest language conflicts in Puerto Rican history. There are, however, other approaches to bilingual education that are rarely considered. The reason is political: the language stakeholders who have dominated the discussion and implementation of educational language policies have benefited from it. English and Spanish language relations reside at the core of the central unresolved political problem in Puerto Rico: the political relations with the United States. Language policies in P.R. have been subordinated historically to political dynamics.

The issue of the educational use of English arose at some point during the administration of all governors since 1969. They all had to face the controversy over the role of English in education and were forced to take stands. Ferré tried to balance the promotion of a new, watered-down Americanization strategy with the defense of the *estadidad jíbara*, or native statehood. Hernández Colón, during his first term (1973–1976) supported the efforts of the Puerto Rican legislature towards a new educational law. The last school laws had been approved in 1903 during Lindsay's tenure, and were more a compilation of existing laws than a unified and coherent pedagogical project. In fact, most of those laws were copies of Massachusetts laws of the time. Hence, a new school law was long overdue. However, the legislative committee did not submit its report until after Hernández Colón was out of office, so its findings and recommendations were ignored by his successor. It would not be until 1990, after Hernández

Colón returned as governor, that a new educational law was finally approved.

The department of public instruction experienced during the 1970s a federalization of its operations (Rey, 2008). There was a significant increase in educational funds granted through federal programs, particularly Title I funds, for schools with low income children, which was the case for about half the public school population in Puerto Rico. The grants provided resources that were badly needed. However, they came at the price of increased involvement of U.S. authorities over educational policies. It also happened in the 50 states. Federal funds were granted with specific instructions over how they were to be used and what kinds of results were expected. Federal programs left little discretion over their use by the secretary of instruction. Hence, as the federal allocations increased their share of the total budget of the department, so did the inherence of Washington authorities over educational affairs. In fact, the same may be said about the government in general, since federal funds in Puerto Rico during the 1970s increased in other key areas, such as health, public works, and welfare programs. Governor Carlos Romero Barceló (1976–1984) named Carlos Chardón (1977) as secretary of instruction because he was known for his success in obtaining federal grants. But Governor Romero Barceló did more than that. He applied pressure against pro-independence movements and attempted to reduce the influence of Puerto Rican nationalism in public agencies and institutions. The political repression reached its climax in 1978 with the assassination by police officers on duty of two pro-independence young men at Mount Maravilla. Also, the Institute for Puerto Rican Culture now focused its attention on universal rather than Puerto Rican culture. He positioned Puerto Rico as an ally of the United States in the conflict over the Soviet invasion of Afghanistan and the boycott of the Moscow Olympics in 1980. Romero Barceló lost a power struggle against the Puerto Rico Olympic Committee, which challenged the boycott and sent a delegation of athletes to Moscow. He played down the importance of the Pan American Games celebrated in San Juan in 1979, for which the audience jeered him at the inaugural ceremonies. Sports teams and cultural organizations that promoted a Puerto Rican identity distinct from the American identity received little or negative attention. Ultimately, conflicts over issues unrelated to language dominated Romero Barceló's administration: a strike at the University of Puerto Rico, the Maravilla killings, union strikes, and the division within the ruling party in 1984.

The department remained a highly centralized agency. Several school reforms addressed this issue and some even made some gains. Two governors, political rivals, approved during the 1990s new school laws that declared the intention to decentralize the education department. Law 68 of 1990 brought several educational reforms, changed the name from Department of Public Instruction to Department of Education, and declared the intention to decentralize the system. Law 68 was amended in 1993 with the creation of the *Escuelas de la Comunidad* (community schools). It appeared that Puerto Rico's educational system was moving fast and with a bipartisan consensus toward a real shift in the locus of policymaking toward the community, particularly the teachers and parents. It soon became evident however, that there remained strong institutional obstacles towards a real decentralization and participation of teachers and parents in public education. The three teachers' unions, AMPR, FMPR and EPA, sent in September 1993 a joint letter to Rosselló with strong criticisms against the reforms, arguing that they could destroy public education. His response, a month later, was distributed through the school system through the chain of command. In it he argued that the needs of the youth should go before "personal egoisms or the limitations of our understanding."

The *Escuelas de la Comunidad* received only modest fiscal autonomy, little say in the hiring of teachers, no involvement in curriculum development, and no say over educational language policies. The community schools decentralized some power away from the central office, but in most cases their decisions required the secretary's approval. Besides, the decentralization ended at the school director's level. The *Escuelas de la Comunidad* considered them the leaders in the educational reform and provided them with much leverage relative to teachers and parents.

School council members were unhappy with the decentralization measures, such as those of the school *La Alicia* in Mayagüez, who in 1997 resigned their posts through an open letter addressed to the school director:

> The School Council is oppressed, persecuted, harassed and coerced by you. The School Council has no participation as it is supposed, in the decisionmaking to improve the functioning of the school; the School Council is not consulted about the need for personnel, like the secretary.

A new organic law for the department was approved in 1999, but left the power distribution intact.

The federalization of the department of education continued into the turn of the twenty-first century and remains an important source of funds and new initiatives for the public schools in Puerto Rico. However, eventually the federalization produced conflicts between the government and federal preferences over pedagogical objectives. For instance, in 2007 Aragunde declined several million dollars from the "Reading First Program" because he believed that the federal requirements to receive them were unacceptable, since they applied techniques to Spanish teaching that were designed for English teaching. *El Vocero*, a San Juan newspaper, reported on its front page that there was a "clash of languages," and that $37.3 million in federal funds would be lost for the program Reading First (26 September 2007).

Administrators and the Bilingualization Policy

Mellado wan an educator who had been involved in politics for several years. He participated in the 1952 constitutional convention representing the pro-autonomy PPD, even though he supported statehood. Later, he joined the PNP and after resigning from his post as secretary of instruction, ran successfully for the P.R. senate in 1972. Mellado knew the politics involved in performing his duties. He knew that his post did not enjoy much autonomy from the governor. Consequently, his educational language policy matched the pro-American ideology of Ferré. He created in 1969 the *Junta Estatal de Educación*, (state board of education), whose members were chosen by the governor and confirmed by the senate (Lopez Yustos, 1997: 207). This board was to formulate educational philosophy and policy, together with the secretary of instruction. It represented a reduction in the secretary's autonomy since it involved the governor directly into the direction and administration of the public schools system. The immediate effects were to create a conflict between the board and the secretary in terms of educational philosophy. The board published a report on its recommendations while Mellado published a separate one. In the end the board did not outlive Mellado's tenure. However, the move represented a paradigmatic shift towards less autonomy for the secretary of public instruction because it expanded the areas of direct meddling by the governor over educational affairs and established a precedent of blunt political intervention. Having become more vulnerable to political changes, the department rapidly became imbedded in the electoral process and the shifts of the two-party system that emerged in 1968.

The department of public instruction offered a coveted prize and a prime target for political rewards. It received one third of the government's budget, plus millions in federal funds. It meant that the party in power could provide many jobs and large contracts to his supporters. On the other hand, the law allowed teachers to take off a semester with salary if they ran as candidates or participated as electoral functionaries. Hence, it was easy and convenient to insert politicians disguised as educators into the school system that could help micromanage the agency. When Mellado arrived at the department, the middle management positions changed hands to members of the ruling party. However, most of the tenured positions were occupied by members of the PPD. The PNP solved this inconvenient by creating new positions to accommodate their followers. The practice of firing opponents and hiring followers became part of the department's culture and increased the size of the bureaucracy. Eventually the non-teaching employees of the department amounted to half of the total employees. Given the politization of the department, the undersecretaries, superintendents, regional directors, and other middle management supported Mellado's plan to increase the English educational use in Puerto Rico after 1969. Mellado believed that most people in Puerto Rico supported his ideas and stressed the importance of participation of non-bureaucratic actors in education. He wrote to the regional directors and the school superintendents about the need to increase the influence of communities through the creation of citizens' committees in the school districts:

> Our public education system demands more effective citizen participation. To that effect I remind you my recommendation about the organization of citizens' committees in each district, made up of the local leadership that can best contribute to the strengthening of the school program. I suggest that this leadership be recruited from the civic, government, professional, cultural, and religious entities that can best serve the public school (Circular Letter 70, 1969).

However, the citizens' committees had no say over policies and were intended to provide support for school initiatives already decided from above. They did not reduce the centralization of the department's decisionmaking. Later, Secretary Ramón Cruz encouraged the creation of citizens' committees and parent-teacher associations, but nevertheless asserted that:

The functions of the citizens' committees should not interfere with the functions of the school personnel. The internal administrative affairs of the districts and regions remain the prerogative of the School Superintendents and Regional Directors by delegation of the Secretary of Instruction (Circular Letter 8, 1973).

The PNP lost the elections in 1972 and the pro-autonomy PPD returned to *La Fortaleza*. Given that the PPD had been a strong language stakeholder against Americanization, Hernández Colón revived a cultural nationalism that favored the Spanish language. Hence, the educational language policy of Mellado's successor, Ramón Cruz (1973–1976) reflected the governor's view and gave little emphasis to the English question. Hernández Colón faced the economic hardship of the 1970s produced by the global rise in oil prices and the decline in world commerce. The English question did not become a major political issue and was not a priority for the governor or the secretary of instruction. Still, Cruz did not reverse Mellado's initiative to create some special bilingual and immersion schools.

The return of the PNP in 1977 gave new emphasis to English educational initiatives. The department promoted the Residential English Immersion Schools, funded with federal grants. Secretary Maria Lacot (1980–1984) wrote in a memo dated November 14, 1983 that:

> The Project of Residential English Immersion Schools is an innovative educational strategy in the teaching of English as a second language. In these schools, English is the instructional vehicle and the language of daily activities. This way, the student will be exposed to it in daily communication.

Lacot referred to English as a second language, even when she promoted the immersion schools. The debate had shifted from the replacement of Spanish by English to the complementation of one with the other. However, the teaching strategy was similar.

Secretary Awilda Aponte Roque (1985-1988) pursued a double policy of showing allegiance to the United States and promoting Puerto Rican nationalist sentiments. She sent memos supporting the campaign to restore the Statue of Liberty and a literary contest sponsored by USA Today about the Bicentennial Celebration of the United States Constitution. On the other hand, the department commemorated the Ponce Massacre of 1937, a historical icon for Puerto Rican nationalists. It also held a literary contest that had to answer why should people buy products made in Puerto Rico. The centralization of the department allowed her to announce in 1985 her controversial plan to reduce the role of English in Puerto Rico's public schools without a public debate. The fact that she did not implement the plan does not deny that she retained the authority to do it.

There was much attention in Aponte Roque's circular letters and memos to the issue of participation by parents and students organizations. The department sponsored in 1987 and 1988 the Congress of Parent-Student-Teachers Organizations (COPEM, in Spanish). Its objectives were to clarify the functions of the school organizations, to integrate those involved at the school level, and to gather their opinion about strengths and weaknesses of the school system. Those two years the department also sponsored two congresses on student organizations. However, neither the parent-student-teachers organizations nor the student organizations achieved any real influence over fundamental educational issues.

Secretary José Lema Moyá (1989–1991) arrived with a discourse about the need to decentralize the department. In his justification for the creation of the *Juntas Administrativas del Distrito Escolar* (school districts administrative boards), Lema Moyá stated that:

> The excessive centralization of the administrative structure of the public instruction system affects the quick processing of the inherent services that support the educational system. Our public school lacks the active and effective participation of the directive personnel at the local level and from citizens in the educational administration (Circular Letter 3, 1989).

However, while the juntas included a teacher and a parent, they were controlled by superintendents and school principals. They had a mandate to give the final approval to curricular affairs without a real power to influence it. Lema Moyá was also instrumental in the approval of the new organic law of the department of education in August 1990. It indicated that the state established the school autonomy as the necessary element in educational excellence. It also stressed the need to create institutions that allowed the participation of teachers and parents in educational affairs. However, the law also gave the secretary the last word in most issues, which became a real impediment for a true decentralization.

Lema Moyá and his successor, Celeste Benítez (1991–1992) did not produce changes in the educational language policy. The arena for language politics shifted in 1991 to the proposed constitutional reform and the elimination of English as an official language. Nonsystem actors took over the issue and education secretaries became marginal participants in the events.

The department of education experimented with a decentralization program under Secretary Torres during the 1990s. He wrote several circular letters and memos regarding the participation of educational stakeholders. He also pursued the involvement of private enterprises by convincing them to "adopt" a school. The biggest reform under his tenure was the creation of the Institute of Educational Reform, which in turn generated the community schools. However, the reform immediately met with resistance form the teachers' unions and soon fell short of its goals.

Aside from all the declarations, Puerto Rico's department of education has remained a conservative institution in which change is difficult by design. No school law has reduced the inherence of the secretary of education over educational policies of all kinds. It also has burdened the secretary with an overwhelming amount of duties, which has provoked an increase in the support staff required at the central office. There is a large amount of bureaucrats in the department who respond to the secretary's instructions with little room for dissent. For instance, by 2004, a letter from the secretary dealing with English in schools would be addressed to the executive associate secretary, undersecretaries, executive director of the Institute for Administrative Capacitation and Advising, assistant secretaries, division directors, program directors, office directors, educational regions directors, English general supervisors, school superintendents, English zones supervisors, English curricular technicians, and school directors. All of them could be removed from their posts by the secretary. Meanwhile, many schools lacked enough teachers, school psychologists, counselors, and even janitors.

Teachers and the Bilingualization Policy

The reduction in autonomy by the secretary of instruction relative to the governor was complemented by a reduction in participation of non-bureaucratic language stakeholders at the central level. This happened by the decline in influence experimented by the AMPR, which was identified with the PPD. However, considerable levels of participation survived due to the sympathies that the teachers' claims had on the public opinion and the increased mobilization and activism that resulted from the creation of the FMPR. The AMPR could no longer take for granted their membership and had to compete against other unions for membership. Thus, the level of participation in decisionmaking within the department dropped only moderately, and language stakeholders within the school system were able to limit the extent of the changes. Even more so, many lower level administrators, still loyal to the PPD, delayed the application of some measures.

The alliance between organized teachers and the government came partly to an end with the creation of a competing teachers' union in 1966, the *Federación de Maestros de Puerto Rico* (FMPR). The *Federación* assumed the strong discourse of a labor union that saw teachers as workers of education. It participated in protests with other workers unions, and joined their picket lines in solidarity. The FMPR became involved in political debates outside the educational realm, such as their public rejection of Rosselló's attempt to amend the Puerto Rican constitution and limit the right to bail in certain crimes. The FMPR also excluded supervisors and principals from its membership, something the AMPR never did. It also criticized the PPD's political hegemony and political project, and its alliance with the AMPR. The *Federación* rose in numbers and competed against the AMPR for teachers' membership. By 2008, three out of four teachers in the public system were members of the FMPR. Its influence reached a peak in 1999 when it beat the AMPR in a vote to select the only authorized organization that could negotiate working conditions with the department. The *Federación* later lost that monopoly after the Commission on Labor Relations of Puerto Rico decertified it in 2008, due to a call for a teachers' strike. At that moment, the FMPR faced the opposition of the AMPR, Secretary Aragunde, and the Service Employees International Union (SEIU), an ally of the American Federation of Teachers.

The *Federación*, as a language stakeholder, supported the use of Spanish as a medium of instruction, rejected plans towards the increase in English educational use, criticized the importation of teachers from the United States, and promoted a larger role for teachers in the formulation of language policies within the school system. Two factors explain the FMPR's preferences: the ideological stance of its leadership and its self-definition as a teachers' union. Its leaders openly expressed adherence to the independence movement. Consequently, they shared the movement's cultural and political nationalist stance that rejected the influence from the U.S. as imperialist. Also the *Federación* defined itself as a union of educational workers that searched for involvement in the formulation of educational policy. It did not only seek liberal union gains, such as better wages and better working conditions in general, but also looked to impinge on some of the secretary's traditional areas of exclusive management, like budget allocations and curriculum development. The law approved in 1998 that allowed public employees to create unions for collective negotiations with the government executives, gave the FMPR the standing of a bona fide union with the sole representation of the teachers at the negotiating table with the secretary of education. Its leadership developed close ties with other powerful unions, like the *Unión de Trabajadores de la Industria Eléctrica y Riego* (UTIER), which represented workers in the energy industry, and the *Unión Independiente de Acueductos* (UIA), for the water works company. The FMPR also created close ties with the independence movement, like the *Liga Socialista* and the *Partido Independentista Puertorriqueño*. Rafael Feliciano, who led the FMPR for several years, attended political rallies of the PIP representing his organization. They all shared in common that the government was the target of their attention. Consequently, they became political actors that could mobilize teachers and impact public opinion, which gave them some leverage over electoral results. That gave them some influence over educational policies, increasing the teachers' overall participation. The FMPR's mobilization and influence increased whenever there was an attempt at bringing back English as a medium of instruction, since their opposition was shared by a large sector of the political spectrum outside the educational system.

The AMPR experienced a different side when the PNP brought down the PPD's predominance to produce the era of bipartisan politics. The AMPR lost the privileged position it had earned, during the PPD's hegemonic years. It now often sided with the opposition and openly rejected the few attempts at bringing back the Americanization policies. It maintained its strategic alliance with the PPD, so its influence increased with every PPD administration, and waned with every PNP administration.

A third organization emerged during the 1990s, *Educadores Puertorriqueños en Acción*, EPA. EPA had a clear adherence to the PNP party and defended Fajardo's Bilingual Citizen Project in 1996. Their adherents were few, even at the peak of the PNP's dominance between 1993 and 2000, and there are no signs that it will grow considerably.

The FMPR initially represented no apparent threat to the AMPR's hegemony over the representation of teachers' interests, both at the policymaking and the public opinion levels. However, the FMPR gradually grew because of its ability to compete against the AMPR in providing material benefits, like the health plan, and its more combative stance against the administration. Their rise came as a surprise to many, considering that the AMPR ran a hospital, a health plan, and a retirement community. The FMPR also offered a more confrontational style of unionism that saw a common cause between their and other workers' struggles for labor rights. Eventually, both unions became rivals for the teachers' preferences, and seldom saw eye to eye on issues relating the school system. The FMPR promoted teachers' strikes in 1974, 1993, and 2008; the AMPR did not support them.

The mere announcement of the 2008 strike provoked the decertification of the FMPR as a teachers' union for several months, with the consent of the AMPR. The FMPR has directed from its inception a strong criticism of the AMPR and has characterized it as one controlled by the employer because it includes school directors and superintendents. The FMPR also rejected the AMPR's affiliation with the American Federation of Teachers. Critics of the FMPR claim that its leadership has a hidden political agenda of promoting the independence cause, regardless of how much it may harm its members. Ultimately, teachers have not been able to speak with one voice due to the antagonistic relations between both organizations.

In spite of their rivalries, both unions always agreed on rejecting any increases in the educational role of English. There were several reasons for this. First, they both supported the cultural nationalism that placed the Spanish language as one of the indispensable components of the Puerto Rican nationhood. Second, they realized the potential costs involved in a reemphasis on English for their membership in terms of retraining, competition from imported American teachers, and loss of classroom autonomy.

The participation of teachers at the central level improved during the Bilingualization period because the benefits of participating increased while the costs decreased. The emergence of new educational unions, including the FMPR and the EPA, but also school principal's unions (*Organización Nacional de Directores de Escuelas*), cafeteria employees' unions (*Asociación Empleados Comedores Escolares*), and others, created an environment where unionization became the norm.

Nonsystem Actors and the Bilingualization Policy

The establishment of educational language policies became more contested since the dawn of the two-party system in 1968. The secretary of instruction lost autonomy to the governor as the department became more politicized. Jobs were granted as rewards for political activists in favor of the party in power, and the bureaucracy of the department swelled. The politization of the department led inevitably to corruption practices. In 2002, former secretary Fajardo pleaded guilty to federal charges of misappropriation of public funds and extortion to enrich him and the ruling PNP. High level educational administrators, included the secretary himself demanded from government contractors, payoffs that went to fund campaign coffers and enriched a few corrupt public servants. Electoral politics and corruption had overtaken the public educational system of Puerto Rico to an extent never seen before.

Political party leaders of the two main parties became language stakeholders on their own. Hernández Colón supported Aponte Roque's plan of 1985 to reduce the educational use of English in the public schools. Barreto (2001) argues convincingly that Hernández Colón's decision to stress the use of Spanish derived from his strategy to deter the statehood pressure arriving from Washington during the late 1980s. In his state of the union address of 1989, President George Bush declared his support for statehood, which naturally stirred the public opinion in Puerto Rico. Hernández Colón took the cause of the anti-statehood movement that included autonomists and pro-independence sectors. The process reached a peak when the U.S. congress held public hearings on a plebiscite bill for Puerto Rico over the political status. It never became a law, but the events polarized Puerto Rican politics around the statehood issue. Hernández Colón assumed the defense of Spanish as a tool to curb the statehood progress in Puerto Rico and Washington. His official language law and his emphasis on linguistic nationalism alienated many voters who went on to support the opposition in 1992. Aponte Roque attempted to establish an educational language policy that was unpopular with significant sectors of Puerto Rico's public opinion. By then, the majority of the population believed that the educational use of English should not be reduced, so it grew no roots.

Ten years later, Rosselló managed to have Secretary Fajardo promote the neo Americanization policy of the Project for the Bilingual Citizen. Rosselló became an influential language stakeholder and supported the increased role of English on the neoliberal concept of globalization, which in Puerto Rico's case meant *anglobalization*. The pro-English discourse now became one of social justice since the globalized era would reward those who spoke the lingua franca over those who didn't. The previous emphasis on cultural nationalism, it argued, masked an elitist program of the PPD to preserve themselves as the traditional economic elite of Puerto Rico. The current global conflict between nationalism and globalization (Laitin, 1993) has, in Puerto Rico's case, served to mask the true essence of the issue: Puerto

Rican versus American identity. The language of the metropolis just happens to be the lingua franca of globalization. What English language stakeholders are really supporting is the colonial language. In the case of Ghana, it was done after independence (Laitin, 1993); in Puerto Rico it was done to prevent it. In the end, Rosselló couldn't convince enough people that English wouldn't kill Spanish any more than it killed the national languages of Ghana (Laitin, 1993).

The Project for the Bilingual Citizen was part of a series of efforts to promote the pro-statehood stance in Puerto Rico. The efforts included congressional hearings over the political status of the island, status plebiscites in 1993 and in 1998, and large spending in lobbyists in Washington D.C. to promote statehood for Puerto Rico. Within this context Fajardo imposed his plan to establish English as a medium of instruction for mathematics and sciences in 1996. It faced a stern opposition from many societal sectors that forged an informal alliance with the AMPR and the FMPR. Nonsystem actors here included the opposition PPD and PIP, important personalities within the academia, particularly from the University of Puerto Rico, labor unions, the *Ateneo Puertorriqueño*, and the *Colegio de Abogados*. It peaked in 1996 with a massive protest in front of the hotel that held a meeting of U.S. Governors. It was called *La Nación en Marcha*, and united most of the cultural and political nationalists (except the PIP) against the attempts towards annexation and against Rosselló's reelection. Rosselló spent much of his abundant political capital trying to make Puerto Rico look more like a state in political and cultural terms. Fajardo's educational approach was part of a larger set of policies that attempted to move Puerto Rico closer to statehood. Fajardo established his project in 1996 but could not make it permanent.

The project was revised and mostly abandoned when the PNP lost the 2000 elections to PPD's Calderón, who named César Rey the new secretary of education. Since Rey identified with the *Hostosianos*, it may have been predicted that he would have increased the educational use of Spanish at the expense of English. He did not. In fact, he followed Calderón's rejection of any proposal to revive the English question. When the Puerto Rican senate produced a study of the language question and debated over new language legislation in 2001, Calderón announced that she would not even consider any bills regarding the issue. Once again, a party controlling both houses and the executive in Puerto Rico, got close to approving educational language legislation but fell short in the end. The party in government in Puerto Rico still relies on the circular letters from the secretary of education to determine educational goals. Circular letters offer decisionmakers some advantages over legislation. It is easier to create a new educational language policy through circular letters than through legislation. It also involves no negotiations with legislators. However, circular letters are also easier to abolish. The result has been a tendency from secretaries to shy away from the issue, except in some cases when the societal conditions provoke the involvement of nonsystem actors into the schools system's language policies as part of larger political projects. Those political projects included Hernández Colón's attempts to block the statehood impulse in congress, and Rosselló's efforts to promote statehood.

The Distribution of Power during the Bilingualization Period

Teachers' unions actively influenced the public opinion in order to improve their working conditions and influence educational decisions. Teacher syndicalism became more aggressive and diversified in negotiations with the administration, some of whom now described it as the *patrono*, or employer. They responded strongly against educational language policies that stressed the use of English and sometimes managed to block them. The teachers' unions also supported policies that increased the educational role of Spanish, particularly Aponte Roque's attempt to retard the use of English until third grade. There was an attempt at creating a teachers' union, the EPA, that would support the pro-statehood stance and hence a larger educational role for English. However, the union was never able to become popular amongst teachers, so its membership remained low.

The institutional change provoked by the increase in syndicalist activity within the department, had an effect over the relative influence over policy of non-bureaucratic sectors. They became powerful pressure groups that increased the political cost of implementing educational language policies they considered unacceptable, like the Bilingual Citizen initiative.

The institutional political nature of the department of education, coupled with the emergence of the two-party system, created erratic and short-lived changes in policies since 1969. The government of Puerto Rico shifted from cultural nationalists to assimilationists every four to eight years. At every shift the party in power promised substantial educational reforms, which went mostly unfulfilled. They changed, however, the emphasis on English teaching several times. Very few policies survived the administrators that implemented them, and most returned to the default state of the department after 1969: the Mellado policy of Bilingualization.

The English language stakeholders in Puerto Rico have yet to acquire numbers large enough to reach a tipping point in which the society seeks a new Pareto equilibrium of language policies (Laitin, 1993). If enough people demand that their children attend bilingual public schools, it will become too costly for the rest not to follow. They would reach a critical mass so large that it would tip the balance. The result would be a new educational language policy with a larger role for English. The Spanish language stakeholders, on the other hand, do not need to overcome the challenges to the coordination of political actions posed by multilingualism (Laitin, 1993). Neither is Spanish an endangered language globally. Spanish is, in fact, a *language killer* itself.

The question would then be whether English stakeholders will reach the critical mass. The answer lies in several considerations. First, the language social use has remained high for various decades, which is likely to increase the promoters of bilingual public education. Also, the pro-statehood movement has established itself as the single largest electoral force for over 20 years. If there is a perception that statehood is possible and near, English supporters will increase. Third, the current migration from Puerto Rico to the United States compares to that between the 1940s and 1960s, which was so massive that eventually there would be more Puerto Ricans living in U.S. cities than in the island itself. Many of those who left returned in the 1970s. The present migratory wave, contrary to the other, includes many professional and skilled workers who are competent speakers of English. So, if this current wave also provokes a mass return migration later on, they will most likely be bilinguals or monolingual Anglophones. That could add enough people to acquire a critical mass of language stakeholders that would increase the educational use of English in Puerto Rico.

The English question would change completely if Puerto Rico were to become a state of the union. The payoff for becoming an English language stakeholder would undoubtedly increase. Statehood would likely provoke the demographic colonization of Puerto Rico. American investors would quickly find out that there is no true entrepreneurial class in Puerto Rico and that capital is scarce. Real estate would seem cheap for U.S. standards. Also, U.S. federal agencies would increase their presence in Puerto Rico, and their businesses would be conducted in English. There would be a great pressure in congress to impose a minimal level of English. At that moment the primacy of the Puerto Rican variety of Spanish could be at risk.

7

The Implications of Language Diversity

The renewal of ethnic conflicts at the end of the twentieth century prompted a resurgence of issues of nationality and ethnicity in the political science field (Esman, 1994; Connor, 1994; Laitin, 1992; Smith, 1986, 1992; Anderson, 1991; Gellner, 1983). The complex nature of ethnicity and nationalism provoked the analysis to move in several directions with various foci. Initial debates concentrated on definitions of nations, nationalism, ethnicity, culture, and other terms that eluded precise definitions but nevertheless had very real effects over millions of people's lives. Other debates concentrated around the effects of ethnic diversity for democratic consolidation, particularly in Eastern Europe and the former Soviet states. There was also an increase in academic journals dedicated to nationalist and ethnic studies. For the most part, ethnic diversity was understood as a problem for democracy and peace, and the Wilsonian vision of each nationality having a state was replaced by debates about the peaceful coordination of many groups' interests within shared political boundaries.

An important element in ethnic and national distinctions is language. The relevance of language for social relations has been recognized by linguists since the development of sociolinguistics, with pioneering scholars such as Ferguson and Fishman. Sociolinguists revealed how language went beyond a tool for social communication to embody symbols representing groups' perceptions of the world. They have also shown that languages may occupy diverse social roles, such as mass communication, official purposes, and business roles. Differences in social use can benefit the social mobility of some ethnolinguistic groups at the expense of others.

Political scientists (Schmidt, 2000; Laitin, 1998, 1992, 1977; Das Gupta, 1970) recognized the implications of language for political dynamics and were influenced by sociolinguists regarding the differences in social roles played by language. Scholars have also shown that many ethnic groups perceive their survival as a direct consequence of preserving their language. However, modern government apparatuses, with their complex organisms, provide incentives for policymakers towards the establishment of parsimonious language policies that limit the number of languages used for official purposes. Hence, demands from ethnic groups on language rights often clash with the interests of states' ruling coalitions, creating tensions that sometimes culminate in repression or armed conflict. Those tensions reside at the core of the political dimension of language.

This book explored the implications of language diversity for political legitimacy and democracy. Language diversity challenges the unity of nation-states, but the institutions developed to meet the challenge may in turn help solidify the legitimacy of governments and democratic institutions. Laitin (1999:4) showed how grievances over language issues "tend to redirect social conflict from the military to the political/bureaucratic realm." Even more so, when language grievances are compounded by religious tensions, the probability of large-scale violence is reduced (Laitin, 2000:533). Thus, an underlying theme of this project is that the successful management of language diversity may be a contributing element in the strengthening of democracies and the unity of multiethnic sovereign states. On a smaller scale, the book examined how educational institutions help nation-states manage the tension between language diversity and government efficiency requirements. The democratization of educational institutions can help solve part of the language diversity challenges, through decentralized and participatory structures. Since educational systems constitute important government organisms, their democratization ultimately contributes to the consolidation of democratic institutions in general.

The book also provided a way to measure a language's social and educational role. It developed the concept of educational language gap as a way to describe and measure the potential differences between social and educational uses of language. Since reducing the gap between the former and the latter is one alternative for governments to manage the tension between language diversity and government centralizing tendencies, the study has focused on the institutions that establish educational language policies. Two key structural features of educational institutions were studied: decentralization and participation. The main theoretical assumption of this book proposed that changes in decentralization and participation affect the correspondence between social and educational uses of a language.

Hence, changes in decentralization and participation were placed against changes in the educational language gap for Puerto Rico between 1898 and 2013, in search of evidence to support, and insights to refine, the book's theoretical argument.

The method used in this book was a combination of comparative historical analysis of various time periods in Puerto Rico with quantitative measurements to illustrate the theoretical approach's universal applicability. Some of the variables measured in this project had no previous systematic means of being quantified, so a big challenge was the determination of accurate and replicable quantification tools for language social use and educational language use. Challenges notwithstanding, the theoretical tools developed through this project provide insights into the dynamics of educational policymaking, and the close study of Puerto Rico's policy changes supports the project's theoretical claims. This concluding chapter summarizes the book's contributions and findings, considers how the theoretical approach can be applied to other countries, and explores additional research areas.

Social and Educational Uses of Language and the Educational Language Gap

The concept of language social use derived from the sociolinguistic debate around Fergusson's concept of diglossia (1959), and its eventual spilling into political science (Laitin, 1992). Ferguson described as diglossic those situations in which two varieties of one language served distinct functions in terms of prestige and formality. Later, Ferguson (1966) described several functions of language and defined the distribution of those functions among two languages in a diglossic relationship. Gumperz (1964) contributed the notion of "verbal repertoires," where individuals use different linguistic forms according to the social role they occupy at the moment. Fishman (1967) and Fasold (1987) expanded the concept of diglossia to apply to two separate languages while Platt (1977) proposed the term polyglossia for several languages.

The sociolinguistic debate entered the political science field during the 1970s. Das Gupta (1970), who also published with Fishman and Ferguson, explored the effects of language differentiation according to social roles in traditional societies, focusing on India. Laitin (1977) studied the impact of language on political culture, and later developed the concept of "language repertoires" (1992), which built on Gumperz's notion of "verbal repertoires." Laitin's "language repertoire" described the number of languages an individual must know in order to take advantage of a state's social mobility opportunities. Laitin later used the notion of "language entrepreneurs" (1999), individuals who become involved in language decisions to help establish preferential treatment for their language in order to maintain or improve their social mobility chances.

One way to understand a country's language repertoire is by establishing the social role of each language used in that country. Using indicators based on population census data, the book established five categories of language social use: primary language, secondary language with primary elements, secondary language, tertiary language with secondary elements, tertiary language, and foreign language.

One area in which a language repertoire is manifested is through education. Educational language policies are important to support or change language patterns. School systems provide a battleground for language stakeholders in their attempts at influencing language social use, through two main areas: as instructional media and as language courses. Both serve to teach the language, but also to instill values associated with that language. For instance, Laitin (1977) found that the use of Somali and English in Somalia produced distinct values in terms of religious and secular values, and tendencies toward competition or cooperation. Since English was associated with secularism and competition, English teaching in Somalia served not only to facilitate the colonial administration, but also to ease the establishment of a capitalist system in which religious values and cooperation would have been less useful than secularism and competition. A similar justification was used to establish English in Puerto Rico in 1900. Various colonial administrators argued that English was associated with democratic and capitalist values while Spanish supported authoritarianism and inefficient economic practices. In their views, English was progressive; Spanish was regressive. The establishment of educational language policies is a political process in which language stakeholders, within or outside the school system, typically attempt to enact their interests.

The comparison between social and educational uses of language produced the educational language gap (ELAG), which measures the distance between a language's emphasis on education and its actual social use.

ELAG = language educational use - language social use

A positive value for ELAG implies a more intense use of a language in education than in its social use, while a negative value means that its social use is higher than its educational use. Diglossic situations tend to produce ELAGs in favor of the high language, which is frequently preferred in education at the expense of the low language, even though the latter is used more widely in society at large. This high/low dichotomy applied to the educational use of English in Puerto Rico between 1898 and 2013, often produced large values of ELAG.

Participation and Decentralization in Educational Systems

The focus on educational institutions stems from the realization that education is a public good, offered by school systems. A mass educational system can help minority groups gain access to social mobility opportunities, depending on the specific shape of the school system. Hence, educational institutions can help solve the challenges of education, but the effectiveness of those solutions is contingent upon the particular configurations of those institutions.

The locus of decisionmaking and the relative inclusiveness of societal sectors in educational policies are two crucial features of educational institutions. They refer to who makes educational policy, and where in the system is it determined. The former refers to the relative influence by administrators, teachers, parents, and nonsystem actors. The latter emphasizes the closeness of decisionmaking to the central educational authority as it moves away to regional bodies, school districts, and ultimately individual schools.

The people involved in educational language policies, termed here language stakeholders, are grouped between system actors (teachers, administrators, and parents), and nonsystem actors (legislators, government officials, politicians, academics, and organized social sectors).

Language stakeholders' interests are diverse, but some general preferences are inherent to their positions. Teachers play dual roles as workers and professionals. As the former, their priority is job security; as the latter, they expect some autonomy within their classrooms. Administrators may occupy varied roles, but the nature of their posts places demands on them in terms of efficiency (by their supervisors) and responsiveness to the schools clients: students and parents. Parents' preferences include a good performance of their children in school, and the provision by the school of social mobility opportunities to their children.

Researchers have shown the many constraints against teacher participation. Still, teachers often become involved in school politics when the payoffs for participation overcome the costs of apathy. One main reason for changing payoffs is the sense of concrete influence on school policies, either at central or local levels. A sense of concrete influence by teachers decreases the probability of being seen as coopted by the administration, reduces threats to career advancement by getting them involved in decisionmaking processes, and provides a sense that the costs of participation are worth the effort. On the other hand, decentralized educational structures are likely to provide incentives for teachers to participate at local levels, while centralized institutions provide greater incentives for larger teachers' unions to push for teachers' preferences. Hence, while decentralization has little effect on teachers' incentives to participate, it influences the kind of participation they will assume. The kind of participation influences teachers' preferences on language policies, where teachers involved at local levels know and experience the social use of their communities' language or languages. Also, if their community's language is a minority language, they are likely to be proficient in it and not have to incur in costs of learning it. At central levels, teachers unions have incentives to simplify policies by reducing to a minimum the number of languages in education. In this sense, teachers unions have a preference towards efficiency similar to that of central educational agencies.

School administrators comprise a heterogeneous group of school principals, district superintendents, regional directors, and central office executives. As managers of the schools' operations, they are driven by efficiency, as are most government managers. However, they receive pressures from their supervisors, from the teachers, from the parents and from the students. Those demands may be contradictory, in which case the administrative level has the potential to influence the administrator's preferences. Communities' demands are stronger for local, more accessible administrators, while central bureaucrats tend to experience stronger pressures from high government officials whose goals are the maintenance and legitimation of the state apparatus. As such, if language diversity is seen as a threat, central administrators face stronger pressures to reduce language use in education than local bureaucrats.

Parents' main educational goals for their children are good performance in classes and their acquisition of skills to improve social mobility opportunities. Parents' participation tends to stem from poor results by their children or by the school. The incentives for parental involvement increase when the poor performance is provoked by bad school policies. However, since parents form a large and diverse group, collective action problems curtail their capacity to become involved. At local levels, their few numbers give them a mobilizing advantage over larger, central organizations. In terms of specific policies, language can be seen by parents as a tool for social mobility in situations where there is more than one language in society and schools can teach their children those languages with the highest social uses. Conversely, those belonging to minority language groups, will also tend to prefer the use of their language in education as a way to reproduce their identity. Decentralized educational structures, where decisionmaking is held closer to communities' levels, are more prone to be influenced by language minority groups than centralized structures. Decentralized structures, coupled with participatory spaces, give language minority groups the best capacity to influence educational language policies.

The effects of decentralization and participation in educational language polices are twofold. First, educational structures that do not offer incentives for teachers' and parents' participation, and that do not reduce administrators' risks in including non-bureaucratic sectors, are likely to produce large values of ELAG in instances where more than one language play a social role. Second, participatory and decentralized educational systems permit the involvement of societal sectors that are more sensitive to local variations in language use and reduce pressures on administrators to follow large-scale efficiency driven language planning.

Puerto Rico: A Case Study

The book focused on the English educational policies in Puerto Rico between 1898 and 2013. The case was chosen for several reasons. First, Puerto Rico belongs to a set of cases, which includes nations like Quebec and Haiti, where official language policies experienced major changes without major regime changes or political crises. Second, the island's political structures since 1898 have developed gradually, which allows for the observation of institutional changes without the need to control for extraordinary external factors. Third, the colonial relationship with the United States provoked the introduction of English in Puerto Rico's Spanish-speaking population, which in turn created some language dynamics similar to those found in multilingual countries. Fourth, Puerto Rico has an unresolved political relationship with the United States, partly because of tensions created by language differences. Such tensions also exist in other regions, like Catalonia and Quebec, so the Puerto Rican case should prove useful in developing generalizable explanations about language politics.

Puerto Rico's population is largely Spanish-speaking, and it lacks the contact and tensions among language groups that are so prevalent in multilingual countries. There is no equivalent in Puerto Rico to the tensions between Yorubas and Hausas in Nigeria, between Chinese and Malays in Malaysia, or Guaraní and Spanish-speakers in Paraguay. However, the use of English in Puerto Rico has experienced a large growth since 1898, which coupled with the imposition of English by U.S. officials in the first decades of the American occupation, provides a base for comparison with societies with competing language groups. The linking of the language question to the political relations with the U.S. divided the island's language stakeholders between pro-Spanish and pro-English and provoked their behavior to resemble that of language stakeholders in multilingual settings. Supporters of the island's inclusion into the American federation understood the need to spread the use of English as a prerequisite to become the fifty-first state. Since their success as a political group depended on the increased possibilities of joining the United States, and the spread of English was seen as a prerequisite for it, their defense of English became linked to their survival as a political entity. Thus, their behavior as supporters of English policies resembled that of language groups elsewhere whose own survival depended on the use of their language. On the other hand, those opposing the imposition of English saw it as a threat to the conservation of the Spanish language and culture, so their behavior resembled that of threatened language groups who resented the imposition of a majority language. In that sense, Puerto Rican language stakeholders understood the need to influence language policies with the same urgency as that of groups in multilingual settings.

This book concentrated on Puerto Rico, but the connection between educational institutions and language policies can be appreciated in other settings. Catalonia is an instance where undemocratic practices blocked the use of a minority language (within the Spanish state), Catalan, while the subsequent liberalization allowed language stakeholders to reestablish their language's prominent role. During Franco's dictatorship Catalan was outlawed from public education in Catalonia and all official affairs were conducted in Spanish. After the end of the fascist regime and the enactment of the 1978 constitution, a nationalist wave swept Catalonia and the use of Catalan in public education became that of a first language. The Catalan ELAG during Franco's rule was large, since it had a social use of a primary language in spite of the ban but played no role in education. After 1978, the

ELAG was reduced dramatically through the reintroduction of Catalan in the school system, turning it into a primary language. The democratic constitution decentralized the Spanish government, liberalized government institutions, introduced Catalonia's self-government (and that of the other *Autonomías*), and opened up popular participation spaces through elections and public accountability of government officials. Those changes affected the educational system by shifting the focus of power from Madrid to Barcelona, and by increasing the overall participation of Catalan society in government institutions.

In Quebec, the decentralized and relatively closed nature of educational policymaking alienated a population sector from language planning. The Charter of the French Language (1977) emphasized the use of French in several areas. The area relevant to this study, education, stipulated that all children of immigrants, who were not already enrolled in English-speaking schools, had to attend schools with French as the instructional medium. The reason was that immigrants preferred their children to learn English over French, due to their perception that the former offered better social mobility opportunities than the latter. This view was expressed in surveys (Endleman, 1995), and was based on the large number of jobs requiring English in Quebec, the preeminence of English in Canada as a whole, and the possibility of migrating to the United States. Thus, the immigrant populations' incapacity to participate in most government decisions allowed the establishment of an educational language policy that did not reflect the social use of English in Québécois society. When left to decide on their own, most immigrant English speakers (Allophones) registered their children in schools with English as the instructional medium. Hence, the large value of ELAG (relative to the use of English) produced by the 1977 language laws was influenced by the centralization of educational decisions and the alienation of minority population sectors. The decline in the educational use of English has in turn affected the language's social use, since a large number of native English speakers (Anglophones) left Quebec to settle in Toronto and other predominantly English-speaking cities, thus reducing the ratio of English to French speakers (Francophones) in the region. Also, the Charter of the French Language imposed the use of French on some aspects of private industries, augmenting even more the social role of French and reducing that of English. Ultimately, then, the decrease in use of English in the private industry may bring its social use close to its educational use, thus reducing the current large value of ELAG.

In sum, democratic institutions offer the best conditions to handle the challenges of ethnic and linguistic diversity. In turn, the successful handling of those challenges by democratic means improves the preservation and legitimation of democratic institutions. Laitin (1998) argued that some of the institutions developed to manage the many political challenges of language diversity may have the unintended outcome of creating or supporting democratic structures. Das Gupta (1998) explored India's federal system and showed how it adapted to the country's cultural diversity by creating a political system based on regional cultural, linguistic, and religious differences. Mazrui (1996) proposed that democracy in African countries could develop stronger if official language policies placed African languages, including local languages, in preferential positions. Since participatory democratic institutions tend to hold more political legitimacy than non-inclusive ones, language diversity, which may appear at first blush to present an obstacle against state cohesion, ultimately may be a force for unity, legitimacy, and peace.

Bibliography

Algren de Gutiérrez, Edith. 1987. *The Movement Against Teaching English in Schools of Puerto Rico*. Lanham, MD: University Press of America.
Anderson, Benedict. 1991 [1983]. *Imagined Communities: Reflections on the Origin and Spread of Nationalism*. London: Verso.
———. 1990. *Language and Power: Exploring Political Cultures in Indonesia*. Ithaca: Cornell University Press.
Arrigoitia, Delma S. 1991. *José de Diego, El Legislador: Su Visión de Puerto Rico en la Historia (1903–1918)*. San Juan, P.R: Instituto de Cultura Puertorriqueña.
Ayala, César J., and Rafael Bernabé. 2007. *Puerto Rico in the American Century: A History since 1898*. Chapel Hill: The University of North Carolina Press.
Babault, Sophie, and Claude Caitucoli. 1997. "Linguistic Policy and Education in Francophone Countries," in Wodak and Corson 1997:159–167.
Bacharach, Samuel B., and Bryan L. Mundell. 1993. "Organizational Politics in Schools: Micro, Macro, and Logics of Action." *Educational Administration Quarterly* 29(4):423–452.
Bainter, Edward. 1914. *Puerto Rico Department of Education Annual Report*. Washington, D.C: Government Press.
Barreto, Amílcar. 2001. *The Politics of Language in Puerto Rico*. Gainesville, FL: University Press of Florida.
———. 1998. *Language, Elites, and the State: Nationalism in Puerto Rico and Quebec*. Westport, Ct: Praeger.
———. 1995. *Nationalism, Linguistic Security, and Language Legislation in Quebec and Puerto Rico*. Doctoral Dissertation, State University of NY, Buffalo.
Barrows, David P. 1907. "Education and Social Progress in the Philippines," *The Annals of the American Academy of Political and Social Science* 30:69–82.
Bates, Robert H. 1988. "Contra Contractarianism: Some Reflections on the New Institutionalism," *Politics and Society* 16:387–401.
Bauch, Patricia A., and Ellen B.Goldring. 1998. "Parent-Teacher Participation in the Context of School Governance," *Peabody Journal of Education* 73(1):15–35.
Bauzon, Leslie E. 1991. "Language Planning and Education in Philippine History," *International Journal of the Sociology of Language* 88:101–119.

Bayrón Toro, Fernando. 2003. *Elecciones y Partidos Políticos de Puerto Rico.* Mayagüez, Puerto Rico: Editorial Isla.
Beadie, Nancy. 1996. "From Teacher as Decision Maker to Teacher as Participant in Shared Decision Making: Reframing the Purpose of Social Foundations in Teacher Education," *Teachers College Record* 98(1):77–103.
Becker, Henry J., Kathryn Nakagawa, and Ronald G.Corwin. 1997. "Parent Involvement Contracts in California's Charter Schools: Strategy for Educational Improvement or Method of Exclusion?" *Teachers College Record* 98(3):511–536.
Benton, Richard. 1991. "Bilingual Education Policy, Past and Future," *International Journal of the Sociology of Language* 88:83–100.
Blase, Joseph, ed. 1991. The Politics of Life in Schools: Power, Conflict, and Cooperation. London: Sage.
Bloom, David E., and Giles Grenier. 1992. "Economic Perspectives on Language: The Relative Value of Bilingualism in Canada and the United States," in Crawford, 1992: 445–451.
Bobonis, Gustavo and Harold Toro. 2007. "Modern Colonization and its Consequences: The Effects of U.S. Educational Policy on Puerto Rico's Educational Stratification, 1899–1910," *Caribbean Studies* 35(2): 30–76.
Bonk, Paul. 1990. *Incentive Structures, Cultural Communities and Ethnonationalism.* Ph.D. Dissertation, Rutgers University, New Brunswick.
Bosque-Pérez, Ramón and Javier Colón Morera, eds. 2006. *Puerto Rico under Colonial Rule.* Albany: State University of New York Press.
Bourhis, Richard Y. 1994. "Introduction and Overview of Language Events in Canada," *International Journal of the Sociology of Language* 105/106:5–36.
Boyan, Norman J., ed. 1988. Handbook of Research on Educational Administration. New York: Longman.
——. 1988a. "Describing and Explaining Administrator Behavior," in Boyan, 1988:77–98.
Bright, William. 1966. *Sociolinguistics.* The Hague: Mouton.
Brock, Sofia and Alan L. Edmunds. 2010. "Parental Involvement: Barriers and Opportunities," *Educational Administration and Foundations Journal* 21(1):48–59.
Brown-Blake, Celia. 2008. "The Right to Linguistic Non-discrimination and Creole Language Situations: The Case of Jamaica," *Journal of Pidgin and Creole Languages* 23(1):32–74.
Brumbaugh, Martin G. 1907. "An Educational Policy for Spanish-American Civilization," *The Annals of the American Academy of Political and Social Science* 30:65–68.
Bryant, Nita. 1998. "Reducing the Relational Distance between Actors: A Case Study in School Reform," *Urban Education* 33(1):34–49.
Burnaby, Barbara. 2002. "Reflections on Language Policies in Canada: Three Examples," in Toffelson, 2002: 65–86.
Cabán, Pedro. 1998. "Americanization, Sovereignty and Citizenship: The United States and Puerto Rico, 1898–1917," unpublished paper, Rutgers University.

Casanova, Ursula. 1996. "Parent Involvement: A Call for Prudence," *Educational Researcher* 25(8):30–32.
Castillo, Alicia and Odette Piñeiro. 2006. "Cambio de roles de los directores de escuela en Puerto Rico," *Cuaderno de Investigación en la Educación* 21:71–90.
Cebollero, Pedro A. 1945. *A School Language Policy for Puerto Rico.* San Juan, P.R: Imprenta Baldrich.
Cioffi-Revilla, Claudio, Richard L. Merritt, and Dina A. Zinnes, eds. 1987. *Communication and Interaction in Global Politics.* London: Sage.
Clampitt-Dunlap, Sharon. 2000. "Nationalism and Native-language Maintenance in Puerto Rico." *International Journal of the Sociology of Language* 142:25–34.
Clark, Victor S. 1930. *Porto Rico and Its Problems.* Washington, DC: The Brookings Institution.
Clune, William H. 1993. "The Best Path to Systemic Educational Policy: Standard/Centralized or Differentiated/Decentralized?" *Educational Evaluation and Policy Analysis* 15(3):233–254.
Coburn, Cynthia E. 2005. "The Role of Nonsystem actors in the Relationship between Policy and Practice: the Case of Reading Instruction in California," *Educational Evaluation and Policy Analysis* 27(1): 23–52.
Cogo, Alesia. 2012. "English as a Lingua Franca: Concepts, Use and Implications," *ELT Journal* 66(1):97–105.
Conley, Sharon. 1991. "Review of Research on Teacher Participation in School Decision Making," *Review of Research in Education* 17:225–266.
Connor, Walker. 1994. *Ethnonationalism: The Quest for Understanding.* Princeton, NJ: Princeton University Press.
———. 1972. "Nation Building or Nation Destroying?" *World Politics* 24(3):319–355.
Cook, Vivian. 1999. "Going Beyond the Native Speaker in Language Teaching" *TESOL Quarterly* 33(2):185–209.
Cooper, Robert L. 2000. *Language Planning and Social Change.* Cambridge, UK: Cambridge University Press.
Corwin, Ronald G., and Kathryn M Borman. 1988. "School as Workplace: Structural Constraints on Administration," in Boyan, 1988:209–238.
Craddock, D., C. O'Halloran, K. McPherson, S. Hean, and M. Hammick. 2013. "A top-down approach impedes the use of theory? Interprofessional educational leaders' approaches to curriculum development and the use of learning theory," *Journal of Interprofessional Care* 27(1): 65–72.
Crawford, James. 1989. Bilingual Education: History, Politics, Theory and Practice. Trenton: Crane Publishing Company.
Crawford, James, ed. 1992. Language Loyalties: A Source Book on the Official English Controversy. Chicago: The University of Chicago Press.
Cruz-Ferreira, Madalena. 2011. "First Language Acquisition and Teaching," *AILA Review* 24:78–87.
Crystal, David. 1997. *The Cambridge Encyclopedia of Language.* Cambridge: Cambridge University Press.
Cuchiara, Maia Bloomfield, and Erin McNamara Horvat. 2009. "Perils and Promises: Middle Class Parental Involvement in Urban Schools," *American Educational Research Journal* 46 (4): 974–1004.

Cukierman, Alex, Steven B. Webb, and Bilin Neyapti. 1992. "Measuring the Independence of Central Banks and Its Effect on Policy Outcomes," *The World Bank Economic Review* 6(3):353–398.
DasGupta, Jyotirindra. 1998. "Multicultural Federalism and National Development: India's Institutional Learning," unpublished paper presented at the APSA Annual Meeting, Boston, MA.
———. 1970. Language Conflict and National Development: Group Politics and National Language Policy. Berkeley: University of California Press.
Deslandes, Roland and Richard Bertrand. 2005. "Motivation of Parent Involvement in Secondary-Level Schooling" in *The Journal of Educational Research* 98(3):164-175.
Deutsch, Karl W. 1966. Nationalism and Social Communication: An Inquiry into the Foundations of Nationality. Cambridge, MA: MIT Press.
———. 1961. "Social Mobilization and Political Development," *American Political Science Review* 55(3):493–514.
De Korne, Haley. 2010. "Indigenous Language Education Policy: Supporting Community-controlled Immersion in Canada and the US," *Language Policy* 9:115–141.
Dion, Douglas. 1998. "Evidence and Inference in the Comparative Case Study," *Comparative Politics* 30(1):127–145.
Dodd, Anne Wescott. 1996. "Involving Parents, Avoiding Gridlock," *Educational Leadership* 53(6):44–47.
Donato, R. and G.R. Tucker. 2007. "K-12 language learning and foreign language education policy: A school-based perspective," *The Modern Language Journal* 91: 256–258.
Duke, Daniel L., Beverly K. Showers, and Michael Imber. 1980. "Teachers and Shared Decision Making: The Costs and Benefits of Involvement," *Educational Administration Quarterly* 16(1):93–106.
Dutcher, Nadine. 1982. "The Use of First and Second Languages in Primary Education: Selected Case Studies," *The World Bank Staff Working Papers* 504.
Eastman, Carol M. 1990. "Dissociation: a Unified Language-Policy for Kenya," *International Journal of the Sociology of Language* 86:69–85.
Ebsworth, Miriam Eisenstein and Timothy Ebsworth. 2000. "The Pragmatics and Perceptions of Multicultural Puerto Ricans," *International Journal of the Sociology of Language* 142: 119–155.
Epstein, Erwin H. 1970. Politics and Education in Puerto Rico: A Documentary Survey of the Language Issue. Metuchen, NJ: The Scarecrow Press.
Epstein, Joyce L. 1993. "A Response," *Teachers College Record* 94(4):710–712.
Esman, Milton J. 1994. *Ethnic Politics*. Ithaca: Cornell University Press.
Esteva i Fabregat, Claudi. 1984. "Ethnocentricity and Bilingualism in Catalonia: the State and Bilingualism," *International Journal of the Sociology of Language* 47:43–57.
Fajardo, Víctor, Isidra Albino, and Nilda C. Báez, et. al. 1997. *Proyecto para formar un ciudadano bilingüe*. San Juan: Puerto Rico Department of Education.
Fasold, Ralph. 1987. *The Sociolinguistics of Society*. Oxford: B. Blackwell.

Fayer, Joan. 2000. "Functions of English in Puerto Rico," *International Journal of the Sociology of Language* 142: 89–102.
Ferguson, Charles A. 1966. "National Sociolinguistic Profile Formulas," in Bright 1966:309–324.
———. 1959. "Diglossia," *Word* 15:325–340.
Fine, Michele. 1993. "[Ap]parent Involvement: Reflections on Parents, Power, and Urban Public Schools," *Teachers College Record* 94:682–710.
Fishman, Joshua A. 2006. "Language policy and Language Shift," in Ricento, 2006:311–328.
———. 1964. "Language Maintenance and Language Shift as Fields of Inquiry," *Linguistics* 9:32–70.
———. 1967. "Bilingualism with and without Diglossia; Diglossia with and without Bilingualism," *Journal of Social Issues* 32:29–38.
Fishman, Joshua A., ed. 1999. *Handbook of Language and Ethnic Identity.* New York: Oxford University Press.
———. 1978. Advances in the Study of Societal Multilingualism. The Hague: Mouton.
———. 1968. Readings in the Sociology of Language. The Hague: Mouton.
Fishman, Joshua A., Charles Ferguson, and Jyotirindra Das Gupta, eds. 1968. *Language Problems of Developing Nations.* New York: John Wiley and Sons.
Fortier, D'Iberville. 1994. "Official Languages in Canada: a Quiet Revolution," *International Journal of the Sociology of Language* 105/106:69–97.
Fuhrman, S. H., and B. Malen, eds. 1990. *The Politics of Curriculum and Testing.* London: Taylor and Francis.
Futrell, Mary Hatwood. 1988. "Teachers in Reform: The Opportunity for Schools," *Educational Administration Quarterly* 24(4):374–380.
García Martínez, Alfonso L. 1982. *Puerto Rico: Leyes Fundamentales.* Río Piedras, P.R: Edil.
Gaziel, Haim. 2008. "Site-based Management: Emergence and Effects: the Case of Israel," *International Studies in Educational Administration* 36 (3): 19–34.
Geertz, Clifford. 1973. The Interpretation of Cultures: Selected Essays. New York: Basic Books.
Gellner, Ernest. 1983. *Nations and Nationalism.* Ithaca, NY: Cornell University Press.
Greenberg, Joseph H. 1956. "The Measurement of Linguistic Diversity," *Language* 32(1):109–115.
Greenfield, William D., Jr. 1995. "Toward a Theory of School Administration: The Centrality of Leadership," *Educational Administration Quarterly* 31(1):61–85.
Grin, François. 1996. "Economic Approaches to Language and language Planning: an Introduction," *International Journal of the Sociology of Language* 121:1–16.
Grosjean, François. 1982. *Life with Two Languages: An Introduction to Bilingualism.* Cambridge, MA: Harvard University Press.
Gumperz, John J. 1964. "Linguistic and Social Interaction in Two Communities," *American Anthropologist* 66:137–53.

Hamers, Josiane F. and Kirsten M. Hummel. 1994. "The Francophones in Quebec: Language Policies and Language Use," *International Journal of the Sociology of Language* 105/106: 127–152.

Hammad, Waheed and Nigel Norris. 2009. "Centralised Control: A Barrier to Shared Decision-making in Egyptian Secondary Schools," *International Studies in Educational Administration* 37(2):60–73.

Hannaway, Jane, and Martin Carnoy, eds. 1993. *Decentralization and School Improvement: Can We Fulfill the Promise?* San Francisco: Jossey-Bass.

Hannaway, Jane, and Marlaine E. Lockheed, eds. 1986. The Contributions of the Social Sciences to Educational Policy and Practice: 1965–1985. Berkeley: McCutchan.

Hebblethwaite, Benjamin. 2012. "French and underdevelopment, Haitian Creole and development: Educational language policy problems and solutions in Haiti," *Journal of Pidgin and Creole Languages* 27(2):255–302.

Hill, Paul T. 1997. "A Public Education System for the New Metropolis," *Education and Urban Society* 29 (4):490–508.

Hobsbawm, Eric. 1964. *The Age of Revolution, 1789–1848.* New York: Mentor.

Hobsbawm, Eric and Terence Ranger, eds. 1983. *The Invention of Tradition.* Cambridge: Cambridge University Press.

Honig, Meredith I. 2004. "The New Middle Management: Intermediary Organizations in Educational Policy Implementation," *Educational Evaluation and Policy Analysis* 26(1):65–87.

Hornberger, Nancy, ed. 2003. Continua of Biliteracy: An Ecological Framework for Educational Policy, Research and Practice in Multilingual Settings. Buffalo: Multilingual Matters, Ltd.

Hornberger, Nancy and Viniti Vaish. 2009. "Mulitilingual Language Policy and School Linguistic Practice: Globalization and English-language Teaching in India, Singapore and South Africa," *Compare: A Journal of Comparative and International Education* 39(3): 305–320.

Huget, Angel. 2006. "Small Languages and School: The Case of Catalonia and the Basque Country," *International Journal of the Sociology of Language* 182: 147–159.

Iannàccaro, Gabriele, and Vittorio Dell'Aquila. 2011. "Historical linguistic minorities: suggestions for classification and typology," *International Journal of the Sociology of Language* 210: 29–45.

International Institute of Teachers College, Columbia University. 1926. *A Survey of the Educational System of Porto Rico.* New York: Columbia University.

Irizarry-Mora, Edwin. 2011. *Economía de Puerto Rico, 2nd edition.* Mexico: Thomson Learning.

Jung, Sook Kyung, and Bonny Norton. 2002. "Language Planning in Korea: The New Elementary English Program," in Tollefson, 2002: 245–266.

Katzner, Kenneth. 2002. *The Languages of the World.* London: Routledge.

Keith, Novella Z. 1996. "A Critical Perspective on Teacher Participation in Urban Schools," *Educational Administration Quarterly* 32(1):45–79.

Kerchner, C. T., and J.E. Koppich. 1993. *A Union of Professionals: Labor Relations and Educational Reform.* New York: Teachers College.

King, Gary, Robert O. Keohane, and Sidney Verba. 1994. *Designing Social Inquiry: Scientific Inference in Quantitative Research.* Princeton: Princeton University Press.

Kloss, Heinz. 1968. "Notes Concerning a Language-Nation Typology," in Fishman, Ferguson, and DasGupta 1968:69–86.

Kohli, Atul, et al. 1995. "The Role of Theory in Comparative Politics; A Symposium," *World Politics* 48:1–49.

Kohn, Alfie. 1998. "Only for My Kid: How Privileged Parents Undermine School Reform," *Phi Delta Kappan* 79(8):568–577.

Kohn, Hans. 1982. *Nationalism: Its Meaning and History.* Malabar, Fla: Robert E. Krieger Publishing Co.

Kuo, Eddie C. Y. 1979. "Measuring Communicativity in Multilingual Societies: The Case of Singapore and Malaysia," *Anthropological Linguistics* 21(7):328–40.

Laitin, David. 2000. "Language Conflict and Violence: The Straw that Strengthens the Camels Back," in National Research Council.

———. 1999. "Language Conflict and Violence: Or The Straw that Strengthened the Camel's Back," *Estudio/Working Paper* 1999/137. Washington, DC: Committee on International Conflict Resolution at the National Academy of Sciences.

———. 1998. "What is a Language Community?" unpublished paper presented at the APSA Annual Meeting, Boston, MA.

———. 1993. "The Game Theory of Language Regimes," *International Political Science Review* 14(3):227-239.

———. 1992. Language Repertoires and State Construction in Africa. Cambridge: Cambridge University Press.

———. 1988. "Language Games," *Comparative Politics* 20:289–302.

———. 1977. Politics, Language, and Thought: The Somali Experience. Chicago: University of Chicago Press.

Laitin, David, Carlota Solé, and Stathis N. Kalyvas. 1994. "Language and the Construction of States: The Case of Catalonia in Spain," *Politics and Society* 22(1):5–29.

Laponce, J.A. 1987. "Language and Communication: The Rise of the Monolingual State," in Cioffi-Revilla, Merritt, and Zinnes 1987:183–208.

Lauglo, Jon. 1995. "Forms of Decentralisation and their Implications for Education," *Comparative Education* 31(1):5–29.

Lewis, Anne C. 1995. "Changing Views of Parental Involvement," *Phi Delta Kappan* 76:430–431.

Lewis, M. Paul (ed.), 2009. *Ethnologue: Languages of the World, Sixteenth edition.* Dallas, Tex.: SIL International. Online version: http://www.ethnologue.com/.

Lieberson, Stanley. 1964. "An Extension of Greenberg's Linguistic Diversity Measures," *Language* 40(4):526–531.

Lockheed, Marlaine E., Adriaan Verspoor, and associates. 1991. *Improving Primary Education in Developing Countries.* Oxford: Oxford University Press.

López-Laguerre, María M. 1997. El Bilingüismo en Puerto Rico: Actitudes Socio-lingüísticas del Maestro. San Juan, P.R: Editorial Espuela.

López-Yustos, Alfonso. 1997. *Historia Documental de la Educación en Puerto Rico, 1503–1970.* Hato Rey, Puerto Rico: Publicaciones Puertorriqueñas, Inc.
Mackey, William F. 1992. "Mother Tongues, Other Tongues and Link Languages: What They Mean in a Changing World," *Prospects* 22:1.
Mady, Callie, and Miles Turnbull. 2010. "Learning French as a Second Official Language: Reserved for Anglophones?" *Canadian Journal of Educational Administration and Policy* 9:1–23.
Maldonado, Norman I. 2000. "The Teaching of English in Puerto Rico. One Hundred Years of Degrees of Bilingualism," *Higher Education in Europe* 25(4):487–497.
Maldonado, Rubén. 2001. Historia y educación: acercamiento a la historia social de la educación en Puerto Rico. San Juan: University of Puerto Rico Press.
Mar-Molinero, Clare. 2000. The Politics of Language in the Spanish-Speaking World: from Colonisation to Globalisation. London: Routledge.
Marshall, Catherine. 1991. "The Chasm Between Administrator and Teacher Cultures: A Micropolitical Puzzle," in Blase, 1991:139–160.
Maurais, Jacques, and Michael A. Morris, ed. 2004. *Languages in a Globalising World.* Cambridge, UK: Cambridge University Press.
Mavrogordato, Madeline. 2012. "Educational Equity Policies and the Centralization of American Public Education: The Case of Bilingual Education," *Peabody Journal of Education* 87: 455–467.
May, Stephen. 2006. "Language Policy and Minority Rights" in Ricento 2006:255–272.
Mazrui, Alamin M. 1996. "Language Policy and the Foundations of Democracy: An African Perspective," *International Journal of the Sociology of Language* 118:107–124.
McGroarty, Mary. 2002. "Evolving Influences on Educational Language Policies," in Tollefson, 2002:17–36.
Meadwell, Hudson. 1993. "The Politics of Nationalism in Quebec," *World Politics* 45:203–41.
Mehta, Jal. 2013. "How Paradigms Create Politics: The Transformation of American Educational Policy, 1980–2001," *American Educational Research Journal* 50(2): 285–324.
Miller, Paul. 1917. *Puerto Rico Department of Education Annual Report.* Washington, D.C: Government Press.
Mitchell, Rosamond, and Myles, Florence. 2004. *Second Language Learning Theories.* London: Arnold Publishers.
Mkilifi, M. H. Abdulaziz. 1978. "Triglossia and Swahili-English Bilingualism in Tanzania," in Fishman 1978:129–152.
Mohrman, A. M., R. A.Cooke, and S. A. Mohrman. 1978. "Participation in Decision Making: A Multidimensional Perspective," *Educational Administration Quarterly* 14(1):12–29.
Morale, Amparo. 2000. "¿Simplificación o Interferencia?: el Español de Puerto Rico," *International Journal of the Sociology of Language* 142:35–62.
Morales Carrión, Arturo. 1983. *Puerto Rico: A Political and Cultural History.* New York: W. W. Norton & Company.

Morales Coll, Eduardo, ed. 2002. *Lengua del estado; lengua del pueblo.* San Juan, Puerto Rico: Librería Editorial Ateneo.
Moravcsik, Edith A. 2007. "What is Universal about Typology?" *Linguistic Typology* 11:27–41.
Moreno Fernandez, Francisco. 2008. "Introduction: a Sociolinguistic Panorama of Spanish in Spain," *International Jourmal of the Sociology of Language* 193/194:13–20.
Morris, Nancy. 1995. *Puerto Rico: Culture, Politics, and Identity.* Westport, Conn: Praeger.
National Research Council. 2000. *International Conflict Resolution after the Cold War.* Washington, DC: The National Academies Press.
Navarro-Rivera, Pablo. 2006. "Acculturation under duress: The Puerto Rican experience at the Carlisle Indian Industrial School 1898–1918," *CENTRO Journal* 18(1): 223–259.
Negrón de Montilla, Aida. 1990. *La Americanización de Puerto Rico y el Sistema de Instrucción Pública, 1900–1930.* Río Piedras: Editorial de la Universidad de Puerto Rico.
Olson, Mancur. 1971. The Logic of Collective Action: Public Goods and the Theory of Groups. Cambridge: Harvard University Press.
Ortega, Lourdes. 2011. Second Language Acquisition: Critical Concepts in Linguistics. New York: Routledge.
Osuna, Juan José. 1949. *A History of Education in Puerto Rico.* Río Piedras, P.R: University of Puerto Rico Press.
Padín, José. 1916. The Problem of Teaching English to the People of Puerto Rico. San Juan, P.R: Department of Education.
―――. 1935. Puerto Rico Department of Education Annual Report. Washington, D.C: Government Press.
Pagán, Bolívar. 1972. *Historia de los Partidos Políticos Puertorriqueños.* San Juan, Puerto Rico: Librería Campos.
Parasher, S.V. 1980. "Mother Tongue-English Diglossia: A Case Study of Educated Indian Bilinguals' Language Use," *Anthropological Linguistics* 22(4):151–162.
Paulston, Chirstina and Kai Heidemann. 2006. "Language Policies and the Education of Linguistic Minorities," in Ricento 2006:292–310.
Pennycook, Alastair. 2002. "Language Policy and Docile Bodies: Hong Kong," in Tollefson, 2002.
―――. 1997. "Critical Applied Linguistics and Education," in Wodak and Corson, 1997:23-32.
Platt, John T. 1977. "A Model for Polyglossia and Multilingualism (with Special reference to Singapore and Malaysia)," *Language in Society* 6:361–378.
Popkin, Samuel. 1979. The Rational Peasant: The Political Economy of Rural Society in Vietnam. Berkeley: University of California Press.
Pool, Jonathan. 1991. "The Official Language Problem," *American Political Science Review* 85(2): 495–514.
Pousada, Alicia. 2010. "English-Speaking Enclaves in Puerto Rico," paper delivered at the College English Association Conference, March 19–20. University of Puerto Rico, Rio Piedras.
―――. 2006. "The Sociolinguistic Implications of Teaching English in Puerto Rico," *PRTESOLGram* 33(3), 6–27.

———. 2000. "The Competenet Bilingual in Puerto Rico," *International Journal of the Sociology of Language* 142:103–118.
Puerto Rico Department of Education. 1903–2012. *Circular Letters*. Unpublished. San Juan, Puerto Rico.
———. 1899–1944. *Annual Reports of the Commissioner of Education*. Washington, D.C: Government Press.
———. 1997. Proyecto Para Formar Un Ciudadano Bilingüe. Unpublished manuscript.
Quintero Rivera, Ángel. 1984. *Conflictos de clase y política en Puerto Rico*. Río Piedras, Puerto Rico: Huracán.
Rahman, Tariq. 1996. "The Punjabi Movement in Pakistan," *International Journal of the Sociology of Language* 122:73–88.
Rata, Elizabeh. 2012. "The Politics of Knowledge in Education," *British Educational Research Journal* 38(1):103–124.
Rey, Cesar. 2008. El reto de la gobernabilidad en la educación pública en Puerto Rico. Madrid: Taurus.
Rice, Eugene, and Anthony Grafton. 1994. *The Foundations of Early Modern Europe, 1460–1559*. New York: W W Norton & Co Inc.
Ricento, Thomas, ed. 2006. *An Introduction to Language Policy: Theory and Method*. Malden, MA: Blackwell Publishing.
Rigual, Néstor. 1967. *Reseña de los gobernadores de Puerto Rico: 1900–1930*. Río Piedras, P.R: Editorial Universitaria.
Rivera, Ángel Israel. 2007. *Puerto Rico ante los retos del siglo XXI*. San Juan, PR: Editorial Nueva Aurora.
Robertson, Ian. 1990. "Some Patterns of Language Use in the Period of Transition from Dutch to British Rule in the Guiana Colonies," *International Journal of the Sociology of Language* 85:51–60.
Rodino, Ana María. 1992. "Language Rights and Education for the Afro-Caribbean English-Speaking Minorities in Central America: Contributions to the Discussion on Bilingual Education in Costa Rica," *La Educación* 20:137–154.
Rodríguez Bou, Ismael. 1960. *Estudio del sistema educativo de Puerto Rico*. Río Piedras, P.R: University of Puerto Rico Press.
Sabater, Ernest. 1984. "An Approach to the Situation of the Catalan Language: Social and Educational Use," *International Journal of the Sociology of Language* 47:29–41.
Samuelson, Beth, and Sarah Freedman. 2010. "Language Policy, Multilingual Education, and Power in Rwanda," *Language Policy* 9:191–215.
San Román Gago, Sonsoles. 2013. "Evolución de los modelos metodológicos y su relación con la política educativa en España," *Educação e Pesquisa* 39(1):227–243.
Schildkraut, Deborah J. 2007. Press One for English: Language Policy, Public Opinion and American Identity. Princeton: Princeton University Press.
———. 2003. "American Identity and Attitudes toward Official-English Policies," *Political Psychology* 24(3):469–499.
Schmidt, Ronald, Sr. 2006. "Political Theory and Language Policy," in Ricento 2006.
———. 2000. Language Policy and Identity Politics in the United States. Philadelphia: Temple University Press.

Schweers, C. William, and Madeleine Hudders. 2000. "The Reformation and Democratization of English Education in Puerto Rico" *International Journal of the Sociology of Language* 142:63–87.
Seidlhofer, Barbara. 2004. "Research Perspectives on Teaching English as a Lingua Franca," *Annual Review of Applied Linguistics* 24:209–239.
Shedd, Joseph B. 1988. "Collective Bargaining, School Reform, and the Management of School Systems," *Educational Administration Quarterly* 24(4):405–415.
Skutnabb-Kangas, Tove. 2006. "Language Policy and Linguistic Human Rights," in Ricento, 2006:273–291.
Smit, Ute. 1997. "Language Policy and Education in South Africa," in Wodak and Corson, 1997:169–178.
Smith, Anthony. 1986. *The Ethnic Origins of Nations*. Oxford: Blackwell.
Smith, Anthony, ed. 1992. *Ethnicity and Nationalism*. New York: E. J. Brill.
Smith, M.S, and J. O'Day. 1990. "Systemic School Reform," in Fuhrman and Malen 1990:233–267.
Solé, Yolanda. 1995. "Language, Nationalism, and Ethnicity in the Americas" *International Journal of the Sociology of Language* 116:111–137.
Solís, José. 1994. *Public School Reform in Puerto Rico: Sustaining Colonial Models of Development*. Westport, CT: Greenwood.
Sommer, Doris. 2003. *Bilingual Games: Some Literary Investigations*. New York: Palgrave Press.
Sonntag, Selma K. 2002. "Minority Language Politics in North India," in Tollefson, 2002.
Sparrow, Bartholomew H. 2006. *The Insular Cases and the Emergence of American Empire*. Lawrence: University Press of Kansas.
Spolsky, Bernard. 2004. *Language Policy: New Topics in Sociolinguistics*. Cambridge, UK: Cambridge University Press.
St. Hilaire, Aonghas. 2009. "Postcolonial identity politics, language and the schools in St. Lucia," *International Journal of Bilingual Education and Bilingualism* 2(1):31–46.
Stewart, William. 1968. "A Sociolinguistic Typology for Describing National Multilingualism," in Fishman, 1968:531–45.
Subtirelu, Nicholas Close. 2013. "'English... it's part of our blood': Ideologies of Language and Nation in United States Congressional Discourse," *Journal of Sociolinguistics* 17(1):37–65.
Teachers' College International Institute, Columbia University. 1926. *A Survey of the Public Education System of Puerto Rico*. New York: Teachers' College Bureau of Publications.
Tollefson, James W., ed. 2002. *Language Policies in Education: Critical Issues*. London: Lawrence Erlbaum Associates, Publishers.
Torres González, Roamé. 2002. *Idioma, bilingüismo y nacionalidad: la presencia del inglés en Puerto Rico*. San Juan: Editorial de la Universidad de Puerto Rico.
Tucker, G. Richard. 2005. "Innovative language education programs for heritage language students: The special case of Puerto Ricans," *International Journal of Bilingual Education and Bilingualism* 8(2–3):188–205.
Tyack, David. 1993. "School Governance in the U.S: Historical Puzzles and Anomalies," in Hannaway and Carnoy 1993:1–32.

Valleverdú, Francesc. 1984. "A Sociolinguistic History of Catalan," *International Journal of the Sociology of Language* 47:13–28.
Vélez, Jorge. 2000. "Understanding Spanish-language Maintenance in Puerto Rico: Political Will Meets the Demographic Imperative," *International Journal of the Sociology of Language* 142:5–24.
Verdugo, Richard R., Nancy M.Greenberg, Ronald D. Henderson, Oscar Uribe Jr., and Jeffrey M.Schneider. 1997. "School Governance Regimes and Teachers' Job Satisfaction: Bureaucracy, Legitimacy, and Community," *Educational Administration Quarterly* 33(1):38–66.
Vexliard, Alexandre. 1970. "Centralization and Freedom in Education," *Comparative Education* 6 (1):37–47.
Vincent, Carol. 1996. "Parent Empowerment? Collective Action and Inaction in Education," *Oxford Review of Education* 22(4):465–482.
Vivas Maldonado, José Luis. 1978. *Historia de Puerto Rico.* New York: L.A. Publishing.
Weinstein, Brian, ed. 1990. *Language Policy and Political Development.* Norwood, NJ: Ablex Publishing Corp.
Weiss, Carol H. 1993. "Shared Decision Making About What? A Comparison of Schools with and without Teacher Participation," *Teachers College Record* 95(1):69–92.
Wiley, Terrence G. 2002. "Accessing Language Rights in Education: A Brief History of the U.S. Context," in Tollefson 2002:39–64.
Wissler, Dorothy F., and Flora Ida Ortiz. 1986. "The Decentralization Process of Schools Systems: A Review of the Literature," *Urban Education* 21(3):280–294.
Wodak, R. and Corson, D., eds. 1997. Encyclopedia of Language and Education, Vol. I: Language Policy and Political Issues in Education. Amsterdam: Kluwer Academic Publishers.
Wong, Kennet. 1994. "The Politics of Education: From Political Science to Multi-disciplinary Inquiry," in *Journal of Education Policy* 9(5):21–35.
Wright, Sue. 2004. Language Policy and Language Planning: From Nationalism to Globalisation. New York: Palgrave Macmillan.
Wyrod, Christopher. 2008. "A Social Orthography of Identity: The N'ko Literacy Movement in West Africa," *International Journal of the Sociology of Language* 192:27–44.
Zentella, Ana C. 2003. ""José, can you see?" Latin@ Responses to Racist Discourse," in Sommer 2003:51–66.

Index

Academia Antillana de la Lengua, 60
Academia Norteamericana de la Lengua Española, 6
Academia Puertorriqueña de la Lengua Española, 13
Academia Puertorriqueña de la Lengua, 60
African-American language group, 6
Afrikaans, 2
American Education Week, 83
American Legion, 83
AMPR. See *Asociación de Maestros de Puerto Rico*
Anglophones, 6, 14, 101, 130, 148, 157
Anglo-Saxon, 6, 99
Aponte Roque, Awilda, 64, 87, 139, 140, 145, 147
Arabic, 10, 22
Aragunde, Rafael, 67, 88, 125, 137; FMPR relations, 67, 142
Aruba, 16-18
Asian language groups, U.S., 6
Asociación de Escuelas Privadas de Puerto Rico, 64
Asociación de Maestros de Puerto Rico (AMPR), 14, 56; and the American Federation of Teachers, 144; and the *Escuelas de la Comunidad*, 33, 136; FMPR relations, 33, 133, 136, 141-144, 146; history, 51-52, 112, 115, 125; and José Gallardo, 85; and José Padín, 55, 107, 117, 119; and Juan B. Huyke, 54, 83, 107, 112, 116, 119; as language stakeholder, 104, 107, 112, 116, 118-120; and Mariano Villaronga, 129; and the *Partido Unión*, 112, 115, 118-119; and Paul Miller, 53-54, 106, 115-116; and the PNP, 143; and the PPD, 59, 129-130, 133, 141-143; and Rafael Aragunde, 142; syndicalist objectives, 114-115, 123; and Víctor Fajardo, 146
Ateneo de Puerto Rico, 13
Austria, 14-15

Bahamas, the, 17
Bainter, Edward, 49, 51-52, 103
Baquero, Gloria, 67
Basque Country, 5
Belgium, 4
Belize, 17
Benítez, Celeste, 64, 76, 125, 140
Bermuda, 17
Bilingual Citizen Project. See *Proyecto Para Formar un Ciudadano Bilingüe*
Bilingual Education Act (1968), 61
British Empire, 10
Brumbaugh, Martin, 49-50, 79, 81, 94, 109, 123
bureaucratic efficiency, 5

Cabot Lodge, Henry, Jr., 58
Calderón, Sila, 67, 146
California, 6
Canada, 13, 18, 81, 157
Caribbean, 17, 18, 69, 74
Carlisle Indian Industrial School, 48, 49
Castile, 5, 81
Catalonia, 5, 16, 18, 155-157
Cebollero, Pedro, 84
Chardón, Carlos, 64, 135
Charter of the French Language (1977), 157
Cherokee, 47
Chicago, 93, 125: school system, 37
Clark, Victor, 48-49, 79- 81
class cleavages, 3-4, 6
cold war, 58
Colombia, 17
Corsican, 15
Costa Rica, 17

Crawford-Butler Law. *See* Law of Elected Governor
Creole: English, 10, 17; Haitian, 7, 17, 22; Jamaican, 17
Cruz, Ramón, 64, 138-139
Cuba, 17-18
Curaçao, 17-18

de Diego, José, 13, 53, 60, 123
de Hostos, Eugenio María, 67. *See also* Hostosiano
Del Rosario, Rubén, 13
Democracia, La, 52
demographic changes, 9-10
Dexter, Edwin, 49, 103; educational language policy, 50, 79-80, 90-91, 94; party politics, 51, 120
diglossia, 21-23, 26, 93, 151
diversity, language. *See* language diversity
Dominican Republic, 17, 60
Dutch, 9-10, 17, 69

Eaton, John, 48-49, 79-80
Educación Moderna, La, 72, 112, 115
Educadores Puertorriqueños en Acción (EPA), 143
el problema del idioma, 51. *See also* the English question
English immersion programs, Puerto Rico, 14, 65, 66, 80, 89, 134, 139
English-only Movement. *See* Official English Movement
EPA. *See Educadores Puertorriqueños en Acción*
Escuelas de la Comunidad, 41, 65, 136
ethnolinguistic groups, 1, 3, 6, 7; minorities, 30; political activism, 10, 21, 26, 31, 149; tensions, 5. *See also* language diversity
European Union, 11

Fajardo, Víctor, 145; educational language policy, 65-67, 88, 94, 143, 146
Falkner, Roland, 100; critics, 50, 52-53, 112, 122; educational centralization, 101; educational language policy, 49, 72, 80, 94, 102, 104; and English social use, 68, 73, 81, 89; as language stakeholder, 13, 79-80, 114, 120; and the *Partido Unión,* 103;
Federación de Maestros de Puerto Rico (FMPR), 33; AMPR relations, 133, 141-142, 144; and decentralization, 67, 136; as language stakeholder, 13, 146; party politics, 143
federalization of education, 62, 135, 137
Ferré, Luis A., 59, 62, 134, 137
Finland, educational system, 14-15
FMPR. *See Federación de Maestros de Puerto Rico*
Foraker Act (1900), 49-50, 103-105
Fortuño, Luis, 68, 89
France, 4, 15
Franco, Francisco, 10, 156
Francophones, 6, 157
French: Canada, 6, 10, 157; Caribbean, 17, 22, 69, 71; diglossia, 22; linguistic colonial policies, 2, 7, 9-10; school system, 14-15

Gaifuna, 17
Galicia, 5
Gallardo, José M., 56-57, 85-86, 93
García Méndez, Miguel A., 59
García Padilla, Alejandro, 68
German, 15, 22
Germans, 47, 74
globalization, 4, 11, 30, 145-146
Great Britain, 4
Great Society, 61
Greek: ancient, 10; modern, 22
Guadeloupe, 17
Guaraní, 22, 156
Guyana, 17
Guyana, French, 17

Haiti, 7, 17, 22, 155
Haitian Creole. *See* Creole, Haitian
Henry, Guy V., 49, 120
Hernández Colón, Rafael: as language stakeholder, 64-65, 77,

95, 139, 145; school laws, 134; statehood opponent, 147
High languages, 22, 93, 153
Hindi, 10, 17
Hindustani, 17
Honduras, 17
Hostos, Eugenio María. *See* de Hostos, Eugenio María
Hostosiano, 67, 146
Huyke, Juan B: AMPR relations, 54, 107, 116-117, 119; educational language policy, 52, 55, 73, 91, 94, 112, 114; first Puerto Rican Education Commissioner, 54, 56; as language stakeholder, 83, 104, 113, 121; party politics, 51, 54, 123

Ickes, Harold L., 85
identity: American, 79, 135, 146; group, 13, 38, 155; national, 5, 52, 99; Puerto Rican, 57, 62, 75, 126, 130, 135
immersion programs. *See* English immersion programs, Puerto Rico
income distribution, 5, 6
India, 4, 8, 10, 16, 31, 151, 158
Indians, American, 48-49, 79. *See also* Native Americans
Indonesia, 4
Insular League of Parent-Teachers Associations, 119
Italy, 4

Jamaica, 17
Japan, 4, 15, 33
Johnson, Lyndon , 61
Jones Act (1917), 53, 72, 104-106, 109, 132

Kenya, 9

language diversity, 4, 44, 154; and political exclusion, 7; in Puerto Rico, 75; rationalization dilemma, 1-2, 12, 14-15,17; state politics, 5, 6, 36, 150, 158
language minorities, 2, 4-5, 18, 30, 39. *See also* ethnolinguistic groups

language rationalization, 1, 9, 42; and decentralization, 44-45; challenge of diversity, 1-2, 12, 14-15,17; in Puerto Rico 107, 120, 129; and teachers' unions, 32
Latin America, 18, 58, 60, 74
Latin, 10
Latinos, 5
Lau vs. Nichols (1974), 61
Law of Elected Governor (1947), 57
Lindsay, Samuel, 49-50, 134
lingua franca, 28, 48, 145-146
linguistic human rights, 11, 14, 21, 26, 42
Low language, 22, 26, 92-93, 153

Mandarin, 10
Mariana Islands, the, 47
Martinique, 17
Maya, 17
Mellado Parsons, Ramón, 13; educational language policy, 62-63, 66, 87-88, 94, 147; as language stakeholder, 137-139
Mendoza, Inés, 57
Mexico, 17, 58
Miles, Nelson, 79
Miller, Paul: AMPR relations, 52-54, 112, 115-116; anti-independence practices, 109; and decentralization, 105-106, 110, 114; educational language policy, 55, 73, 82, 91, 93-94, 100; and the Jones Act, 104; as language stakeholder, 49, 54, 83-84, 90, 103, 121
Moreno, Eduard, 68, 89
Muñoz Marín, Luis: cultural nationalism, 57-58, 76, 121, 126, 129-130; daughter politician, 65; economic policy, 121; first elected Governor, 125; political repression, 131; Spanish language defense, 61
Muñoz Rivera, Luis, 123
Muñoz, Victoria, 65

Nahuatl, 17,
National Education Association of America, 83

Native Americans, 5, 47-48. *See also* Indians, American
Nicaragua, 10, 17
Nigeria, 16, 156
Norway, 4

Official English Movement, 6, 13, 42
Official Languages Act (1902), 71, 76-77, 126
Oliveras, Cándido, 60-61, 87, 128

Padín, José, 53, 84; AMPR relations, 117-119; and decentralization, 106, 108; educational language policy, 55-57, 85, 94, 100, 122; as a language entrepreneur, 73-74, 84, 92, 107, 121
Pakistan, 2, 7
Panama, 17
Papiamento, 17
Papua–New Guinea, 4
Paraguay, 22, 31, 156
Parti Québécois (PQ), 13
Partido Independentista Puertorriqueño (PIP), 13, 58, 131, 143, 146
Partido Nacionalista Vasco (PNV), 13
Partido Nuevo Progresista (PNP): AMPR relations, 143; electoral politics, 13, 59, 137-138, 145-146; as language stakeholder, 62, 65-66, 131, 139
Partido Popular Democrático (PPD): AMPR alliance, 59, 133, 141, 143; and cultural nationalism, 57-58, 62, 95, 126-127; and decentralization, 138, 142; electoral politics, 65, 67-68, 121, 129-130, 137, 139; as a language entrepreneur, 13, 66, 131-132, 139, 145-146; and migration to the U.S., 125; Washington relations, 131
Partido Republicano (PR): electoral politics, 50, 85, 119; as language stakeholder, 52, 55-56, 74, 122
Partido Socialista Obrero (PSO), 55, 68, 74, 122

Partido Unión: AMPR alliance, 52, 56, 112, 115, 118-119; electoral politics, 50-51, 103, 121; as language stakeholder, 13, 74, 104, 120, 122
Patois, 17, 81
Philippines, the, 2, 9, 31, 47-48, 100
Piñeiro, Odette, 68
PIP. *See Partido Independentista Puertorriqueño*
PNP. *See Partido Nuevo Progresista*
political participation, 5, 38
political socialization, 3
polyglossia, 22, 151
Portuguese, 9-10
Powell, Clayton, 61
PPD. *See Partido Popular Democrático*
Pratt, Richard Henry, 79
print-capitalism, 3
Proyecto Para Formar un Ciudadano Bilingüe, 66, 88, 95, 143
Punjabi, 7

Québec, 18, 26, 156; language policies, 6, 10, 16, 155, 157
Quintero, Angel, 61, 87, 125, 128

Ramey Air Base, 74
Reading First Program, 67, 137
Republicanos. See Partido Republicano
Residential English Immersion Schools, 139
Rey, César, 67, 88, 94, 146
Rivera Sánchez, Jesús, 68
Román, Rafael, 68
Roosevelt Roads Naval Base, 74
Roosevelt, Franklin, 56, 85, 93, 118, 121
Roosevelt, Theodore, 50
Roosevelt, Theodore, Jr., 107, 121
Roqué, Ana, 72
Rosselló, Pedro: as language stakeholder, 63, 65, 95, 145-147; teachers relations, 136, 142
Russian, 10

Sánchez Hidalgo, Efraín, 60, 87, 127
Sánchez Vilella, Roberto, 128-129

Sandinistas, 10
Sanskrit, 10
School Laws, Puerto Rico: (1899), 49, 97, 102, 111, 120; (1901), 98, 102-103; (1903), 101, 122-123, 132, 134; (1990), 136
Sellés, Gerardo, 55, 119
Senegal, 7
Slovenia, 11
social mobility, 23-24, 149, 152; and diglossia, 26, 90; and education, 4, 13, 38-39, 153-155; and English, 11, 157; and English in Puerto Rico, 18, 65, 67, 75, 92-93, 134
Society Bishop Arizmendi, 61
Somoza, 10
South Africa, 2, 31
South Korea, 11
Spain: education, 42, 97; language minorities, 4-5, 10, 18; language stakeholders, 13, 31
Spanish-American War. *See* Spanish–Cuban–American War
Spanish–Cuban–American War, 18, 47, 97
Sranang Tongo, 17
St. Maarten, 17
Standard English, 5
Subcommittee of the Committee on Territories and Insular Affairs, 86
Suriname, 17
Swahili, 2, 9
Sweden, 4
Switzerland, 4, 14-15, 22

Tanzania, 2
Teachers' College of Columbia University, 54

The English question, 61, 65-66, 68, 74, 148; causes, 69; party politics, 93, 130, 139, 146. *See also el problema del idioma*
The Porto Rico Progress, 52
Title I federal grants, 135
Title VII federal grants, 61-62
Tito, 5
Torres, José Arsenio, 65, 125, 141
triglossia, 22
Trinidad and Tobago, 17-18

U.S. Virgin Islands, 17, 121
U-boats, Caribbean, 74
Unionistas. See Partido Unión
United Nations Resolution 748 (1953), 58
United Nations, 58; language rights declaration, 26; self-determination stance, 121
Urdu, 2, 7

Venezuela, 17
verbal repertoires, 22-23, 151
Villaronga, Mariano: AMPR relations, 129; centralization, 59, 127, 132; educational language policy, 57, 60-61, 86-87, 100, 130; and English educational use, 87, 94; as language stakeholder, 13, 121, 126, 131

Winthrop, Beeckman, 50-51, 120
WIPR/WIPM, 60-61
Wolof, 7
World War I, 114, 117, 121
World War II, 15, 48, 74, 124

Young People's English Clubs, 83
Yugoslavia, 5, 3

About the Book

How have colonial and partisan politics in Puerto Rico affected the language used in public schools? What can we learn from the conflict over the place of English in Puerto Rican society? How has the role of English evolved over time? Addressing these questions, Jorge Schmidt incisively explores the complex relationships among politics, language, and education in Puerto Rico from 1898, when Spain ceded the island to the United States, to the present.

Jorge R. Schmidt is associate professor of political science at the University of Puerto Rico, Mayagüez.